Improve Your People Skills:

How to Build Relationships Anywhere, with Anyone, in Any Situation

By Patrick King
Social Interaction and Conversation Coach at
www.PatrickKingConsulting.com

Table of Contents

Chapter 1: Build Your Social Awareness

Are you one of those people that loathes small talk, considers themselves an introvert and wouldn't dream of striking up a conversation with a stranger at a bus stop? Perhaps you're the type who constantly finds they accidentally offend others, or that every other interaction feels a bit "off" somehow. Or maybe you're just aware of the fact that in our world today the conversational arts seem to be in decline, and you'd like to make an effort to be more charming, more likeable, better understood and more socially connected to people.

Whatever your current social stumbling blocks are right now, the material covered in this book will help you master one of life's most challenging subjects: other people! In the chapters that follow we won't just look at easy tricks and hacks to use to make you more confident and engaging. We'll also look at *why* these approaches work, and the underlying mindset shift that's required to become a charismatic, cooperative and genuinely likeable person, socially.

We'll explore practical ways to start fine-tuning your social perceptions and awareness, to begin strengthening your empathy muscle, to make small tweaks to your language so that other people really *get* what you're saying, how to listen, how to assert your own boundaries, argue effectively, apologize when necessary and, trickiest of all, navigate those situations in life when communication breaks down and you have a conflict on your hands.

Even if you consider yourself socially awkward and hopeless in conversation, rest assured that there *is* a version of you that is confident, likeable and socially at ease, and getting there is just a matter of understanding a few basic principles and applying them to your everyday life. Strengthen these skills even a little and you will find the rewards are immense. The right people skills can completely change your life – whether professionally or personally, it's hard to imagine a situation that isn't improved with a little more tact, charm and skillful communication!

The Triangle Eye Contact Technique

There are so many "people skills" to master and so much to learn that it can be difficult to know where to start. One easy place to begin: the eyes. Even those of us who find socializing difficult know that body language is the foundation of all other language. Arguably, of the entire body, our gaze and where we rest our eyes is the most important.

Yet so powerful is eye contact that not doing enough can make an entire interaction feel cold and detached, while doing a fraction of a second too much can make that same interaction feel "creepy" or off somehow. The goal with eye contact is to ensure you're *connecting* with the person in front of you in a very primal, nonverbal way, without that connection feeling too intense or awkward. How?

The "triangle technique" is one approach that promises to help. The idea is that this will make the other person feel that you are engaged in what they're saying, but you'll avoid dwelling too long and making people feel weird!

Career expert Kara Ronin has this to say about the triangle technique:

> "If you feel a bit awkward staring into someone else's eyes, try this little trick: **Draw an imaginary inverted triangle on the other person's face around their eyes and mouth. During the conversation, change your gaze every five to ten seconds** from one point on the triangle to another. This will make you look interested and engrossed in the conversation" (*The Muse, "4 Reasons Why You Don't Get Noticed at Networking Events"*).

Does it work? Yes! But not for the reasons you might think. Using the triangle technique will actually help you feel more focused and less awkward as you talk to someone, especially if eye contact is something you struggle with. If you feel less awkward, that means you'll convey more relaxation and ease, which the other person will pick up on, and respond to.

Have you ever been talking to someone when you suddenly became aware of the fact that you were staring into one another's eyes? Depending on the context, this might have felt acutely uncomfortable or embarrassing, and one of you might have quickly looked elsewhere—cue all those awkward feelings. This is exactly the situation where you can use the triangle technique to its best. If you notice that there has been some suddenly intense eye contact, relax and simply shift your gaze to the other eye or the mouth. You show that you're still connected and paying attention, but you're switching off that glare of direct eye contact.

What you don't want to do is be rigid about following this rule—which isn't a rule at all. If you're getting hung up on counting five seconds before methodically switching to the next triangle corner, you can expect to create awkwardness, not avoid it! Instead, fall back on this technique whenever you are feeling a little flustered or uncomfortable in a conversation and eye contact is the reason.

Try not to avoid eye contact or seek it out relentlessly—both lead to awkwardness. Instead, think of eye contact like a muscle during a workout. Both can't be active or tense continuously, or they get fatigued. Instead, focus, then take a break. If the triangle technique is still not relieving some awkwardness for you, give yourself permission to occasionally gaze off to the side or down, but if your goal is to connect with the other person, remember to keep coming back to eye contact with them. Keep it light and dynamic, shift your gaze to a new place roughly every five or ten seconds, and relax. One more tip: very few moments of slight awkwardness can't be dispelled with a quick and generous smile!

Using Proxemics

We know that body language matters. For example, most people might guess that if someone is laughing, smiling, and leaning in toward another person, then this communicates friendliness and warmth, right? However, if someone laughed, smiled, and leaned in just a few inches from a stranger's face, most people would interpret this body language very differently!

Proxemics is an important aspect of body language that is often underestimated. Simply put, the term was coined by anthropologist Edward Hall (Hall et. al., *Current Anthropology*, 1968) to describe the amount of physical space that people felt comfortable with when engaging with others. We can use the understanding of **proxemics as a nonverbal way to become more socially aware, and to communicate and decode other people's intentions.**

Hall identified four main proxemic "zones" of increasing intimacy: public space, social space, personal space, and intimate space.

As an anthropologist, Hall was interested in the fact that certain cultures and groups seem to have different preferences. For example, Latin Americans and those living in cities are comfortable standing closer to one another, while East Asians or rural farmers prefer standing a little ways back. There are naturally individual differences, too, and people's preferences may change depending on social context or even the time of day or season in the year. Let's take a closer look at the zones:

The Intimate Zone
Physical contact to around eighteen inches apart
Lovers, family members, and very close friends. Also common during sports!

Stepping into this space is essentially saying, "I'm seeking more intimacy." This can be a flirtatious cue or, in the case of interrogations, a threat designed to provoke anxiety. Be extremely careful deliberately moving into this space. Your intentions will almost always be viewed as inviting sexual or romantic escalation (which may not be reciprocated!) or a not-so-subtle power move designed to literally get in someone's face. So, unless you are already on close terms with the person or have very good reason to believe they'd welcome the escalation, stay out of this zone.

Personal Space
Between one and four feet apart
Friends and close, harmonious relationships

This is the comfortable zone in which friendly and warm relationships are played out. However, there are some gender differences. Whether these are down to biology or socialization is an ongoing debate, but it generally appears that women tend to stand closer to other women than they do to men. This strongly suggests that between men and women, negotiating the sexual element usually means keeping a little more distance, just for good measure!

People who stand closer to others are in general perceived as warm, trustworthy, and likeable, but it's probably more a question of matching your distance to the other person's comfort level. It's not that distance or closeness alone signal anything; rather, welcome closeness will be felt as warmth, and unwelcome closeness will be felt as intrusion. How can you tell?

Pay attention. Try body language expert Joe Navarro's "shake and wait" technique when you meet someone new:

1. Greet them and immediately lean in
2. Give them a handshake (or other greeting if handshakes are inappropriate)
3. Maintain eye contact and a friendly smile if appropriate
4. Take a small step back again and wait to see the effect you've had (Joe Navarro, *What Every Body is Saying*, 2008).

As a rule, if the other person actively comes closer to you, they're comfortable and you can match this by moving in. If they take a step back or angle their body away from you, they might need a little more space, so subtly move back a little or mirror their turned-away posture. If they stay where they are, assume they're happy. Later, when you know them better and if you want to, you can lean closer and observe their reaction. A good rule of thumb is to never continue encroaching or closing distance if you have not received any signal that it's welcome.

The Social Zone
Around four to twelve feet apart
People walking down the street, or during business and social events

This is a neutral, very comfortable space, but it's not as warm and friendly as personal space. So, you're unlikely to cause offense here, but you're also unlikely to make any strong connections.

The Public Zone
Twelve feet apart or more
Strangers and people sharing a public place

At this distance, people are barely interacting at all, and most towns and cities buzz along on the premise that people can enter and leave one another's orbit almost without registering it.

So, how can we use proxemics to improve our people skills? First, you have to understand Hall's main finding, which was that **people manipulate social distances as a way to regulate their social stimulation.** Basically, we moderate our *psychological closeness* by changing our *physical closeness* to others (our proximity). This means that you can use physical distance to:

1. Understand what other people want from you and your social interaction
2. Make others understand what *you* want from the interaction

So, for example, if we are dating someone we're really interested in, we can read their body language by noticing that, as time goes by, they're moving closer and closer to us. We can infer that they are getting psychologically more comfortable with us. But we can also signal our own intentions by moving close and observing the reaction we get. Maybe every time you move a few inches closer, they subtly move that same distance away from you. Even though they never *verbally* tell you, "I'm not really interested in progressing things with you," their body language is crystal clear!

A few caveats here, though. No single body language act or gesture is definitive; before we jump to any conclusions, we need to take in as much information as possible and look for *consistent patterns* of behavior, as well as consider context. So, if the other person is from a culture that favors bigger personal spaces and more traditional or distant dating practices, their failure to lean in when you do might signal very little of their intentions. Likewise, a woman leaning in when you're in a tiny elevator and it's extremely cold is probably not signaling keen interest just because she's standing close to you!

Perceptual Positions for Empathy and Awareness

Social awareness is the bedrock of mastering good people and communication skills. Without awareness of both ourselves and others, we are completely lost and will seldom make genuine and enjoyable connections with others. "Perceptual positions" is an approach that comes from the world of Neurolinguistic Programming, or NLP. In their 2009 paper, Andreas &

Andreas outline what perceptual positions are and how they allow us to do three things:

1. Better understand our own perceptions of the world
2. Better understand other people's perceptions (i.e., have empathy!) and so gain deeper insight into relationships, conversations, and situations
3. Better understand the objective world (*Journal of Consciousness Studies*, vol. 16, 10-11)

Later in this book, we'll consider all sorts of social skills, such as good listening, conflict resolution, strengthening emotional intelligence, and even just the dark art of small talk. But all these skills rest on our ability to be aware of ourselves and others, so that's why we'll start with the awareness-building exercises of perceptual positions.

According to the Andreas & Andreas paper, there are three basic positions that we can take in any situation:

First position: seeing the world through our eyes

Second position: seeing the world through someone else's eyes

Third position: seeing the world through a neutral observer's eyes

Each of us has a "map of the world" that includes our beliefs, values, assumptions, needs, and so on. When you view the world through your perspective, the facts are colored by these beliefs. At any time, we can choose to switch between our own map of the world and someone else's. The third, neutral position is about looking at things without beliefs, values, and biases at all—as much as is possible, that is.

You will become a better communicator and improve your social skills if you are able to flexibly shift between these perceptual positions, i.e., be aware of *all* perspectives in a situation and not just your own. This technique allows a three-dimensional understanding of situations and opens you up to much more information, understanding, and empathy. One caveat: genuinely and cleanly switching perspectives does take some practice, especially if you're not used to it. You will only bring more conflict and confusion to interactions if you only *think* you've changed perspectives but have really just dug your heels deeper into your own!

How can we use this model to improve our social skills? There are a few ways. First, we can use the framework to retrospectively look at situations that have already passed or which are not currently unfolding; for example, a tense situation at work. You can do a "postmortem" on the situation by actively inviting yourself to switch perceptual positions.

Step 1: Take first position and ask yourself some questions:

What's the problem?

What are you thinking and feeling? Can you identify any thoughts, beliefs, assumptions, or biases? How are you explaining this situation to yourself? What are your needs here and are they being met? How are you interpreting events or other people's actions?

When you're done fleshing out your own position, go to step 2: **adopting the second position**. Ask the same questions. However, answer them *as though you were the other person*. For example, don't say, "They think they're always right," (this is really first position!) but rather, "I feel quite certain about what I know," (spoken from *their* perspective).

Again, explore thoughts, feelings, assumptions, fears, needs, and interpretations, but from inside the other person's perspective. Start sentences with "I" and don't rush or put words into their mouths. Next, **step 3 is to go into the neutral position**. Zoom all the way out and pretend you're a neutral outsider looking at both first and second positions with no emotional attachment to either. What is the relationship you see? What is happening and why?

When you've explored all three positions, "shake it off" and come back to your normal everyday perspective. Ask yourself which position was most difficult to occupy and why. See if you have discovered any new insights into the situation. Have you been making assumptions? Are there things you don't actually know? Maybe you can see something you hadn't considered before, or a new cause for a problem is emerging.

With this exercise, it's really important to make a proper break between perspectives. You can do this by literally standing up, stretching, exhaling, or moving to a different body posture or place in the room. Let go of any ego that wants you to blame, judge, or find fault. Instead, just try to be curious and genuinely seek to try on the perspective of someone else. Ask what they would think and feel, not what *you think* they would think and feel—big difference! This means that you may find yourself doing something you never have before—actively considering a point of view that you don't agree with or which doesn't actually make sense to you.

Congratulations! You're beginning to develop empathy and social awareness.

In the example of a conflict at work, you may find the following:

First position: I feel attacked and undermined by the feedback I got.

Second position (a manager): I feel like I'm just doing my job and telling people how they can improve.

Third position: This is a pretty normal interaction, but it seems like there's not a lot of rapport between these two people.

The insight here is to understand that your feelings of being attacked are not the full picture. The next time you talk to your manager, instead of saying, "You've been really mean to me with this feedback," you can try to acknowledge their position by saying, "I know you're only doing your job and want to help me improve, but I felt a bit upset by this feedback." This way you solve the problem in an expanded way and develop the much-needed rapport.

You might be wondering if this approach is only good for resolving conflicts (which we'll explore in more detail in our final chapter). It isn't! Switching perceptual positions is something you can do any time, and in small ways, even as interactions are unfolding.

If you're having a hard time connecting with or understanding the other person, quickly reframe things and ask, "What position are they in right now?" While some naturally empathic people do this automatically, the truth is that most of us are not as good at it as we think. Even a brief moment of reframing can show us that others don't necessarily know what we know, think what we think, feel what we feel, or want what we want. Even if we don't fully grasp their position, just knowing that it's not the same as ours can be a massively useful insight!

This technique underpins so many others. and can be combined with them. For example, let's say you're a man trying to flirt with a woman you're interested in, but you notice she keeps avoiding eye contact and turning her body away from yours despite flirting with you the day before. You very quickly put yourself in her shoes and see what she might be thinking, feeling, and perceiving. Doing so, you realize that today you're talking in a busy public space at night whereas yesterday you were in a relaxed, secluded space during the day. You combine your understanding of proxemics, eye contact, and perspective-switching to realize that she hasn't suddenly lost interest; she's just a little uncomfortable in the current environment. Nothing has changed here— but you have become more aware of yourself and of others, and that makes all the difference.

Three-Step Active Listening: Paraphrase, Clarify, and Summarize

In talking about body language and proximity, you could be forgiven for thinking that good social interactions were somehow mysterious and governed by unspoken gestures that you had to work hard to decode. But of course, people have one brilliant advantage: we can speak! Arguably the only reason humans evolved language was so that we could effectively communicate our perspectives to others without them having to guess.

Active listening will turbo-charge your social awareness skills. People communicate almost constantly, and they share almost everything you could want to know about them. The trick is, though, that we really need to know how to *listen* to what they're saying. It's an amusing irony that some people who are very interested in reading subtle body language cues often miss out on the really obvious words coming directly from people's mouths . . .

"Active listening" is a bit like driving— everyone thinks they're above average! The truth is that genuinely listening to another person takes effort and practice, and most of us are pretty bad at it. It's not just giving the impression that you're paying attention. It's *genuinely, sincerely* taking in what you're being told and putting the focus of your attention on that person so that you can deeply understand what they are trying to convey.

One big thing that gets in the way of genuine understanding is assumed understanding— i.e., we don't listen all that well because we think we already know what's being said. Another major problem is when we judge or evaluate what we hear. Good listeners listen primarily so they can connect and understand, *not* so they can decide if they agree, or what they think of the person speaking.

Brandy Haley and colleagues conducted a study in 2017 where they discovered that nurses who were better at active listening were also more empathetic, and this empathy was connected to a boost in patient outcomes (*NursingPlus Open*, vol. 3). In a study with 115 participants, Castle Bell and colleagues discovered that those on the receiving end of active listening overwhelmingly claimed to feel more understood and even "perceived the [active listener] to be more socially attractive than participants who received simple acknowledgements" (*International Journal of Listening*, 2014).

How do we achieve this same outcome? Here are some conventional active listening strategies people usually recommend:

- As you listen, consciously resist trying to think of what you'll say when they stop talking.
- Wait a few seconds after they stop so you don't come across as rushing in to say your own thing. Take time to absorb what they've said.
- Don't assume people think or feel the same as you, or that their values are the same (see perspective-switching above).
- Don't pretend you understand them when you don't.
- Don't interrupt.
- Avoid cliches like saying "Oh, I totally understand" when you don't sincerely mean it.

These are all really good suggestions, but even still, if any of them are followed with the intention of only *appearing* to be a good listener without actually being one, then you're still going to fail. The goal is not to improve yourself by being perceived as a better listener. To achieve the results we see in countless studies, the goal is to genuinely understand the person in front of you better.

This means that there's really just one main rule to being a better listener: get yourself out of the way!

There's a practical way to do this: paraphrase, clarify, and summarize:

Paraphrasing is repeating what you've been told but in your own words.
Clarifying is asking questions to confirm that you've understood what you've been told.
Summarizing is condensing the essence of what you've been told into a summary that reflects their message back to them.

If you consistently do these three things, you will be well on your way to mastering active listening—and the other person will notice and feel more heard and seen. But again, these three actions are really just a way to demonstrate that we have taken ourselves and our own ego out of the picture so that we can more effectively perceive and understand the other person.

Here's how a conversation looks without active listening:

A: I feel like you're picking apart everything I do, and that I can't do anything right.

B: That's ludicrous. I never do that. I'm very fair.

A: But your feedback was really harsh, and you didn't give that feedback to anyone else. I feel like—

B: Look, I know you're feeling upset, but you're making a really big deal out of this. You don't want me to give you feedback again, fine, I get it.

A: That's not what I said.

Can you identify the judgment, the interrupting, the glib and meaningless reassurance, and the total misinterpretation of what is being said? Here's the same again with active listening:

A: I feel like you're picking apart everything I do, and that I can't do anything right.

B: I'm really surprised to hear that. Why do you feel this way?

A: I think your last feedback was quite harsh, and I noticed you didn't give that feedback to anyone else. I feel like I've almost been singled out.

B: So if I understand you correctly, you're saying you feel as though I'm being unfairly critical and that I'm not that critical with others?

A: Yes, exactly.

B: Is this something you've recently noticed or is this an ongoing problem?

A: Well, to be fair, it was only once with this most recent feedback.

B: Okay, I see. So it seems like you're unhappy with how I've managed this last feedback, and you've come to talk to me about it.

Can you identify the paraphrasing, clarifying, and summarizing above? Importantly, active listening won't magically make problems or conflicts go away, but what it will do is allow people to engage with those conflicts *without jeopardizing the harmonious connection between them*. It makes sense that you can only move forward from misunderstanding or conflict if you actually understand where the other person is coming from. Similarly, you can only really develop intimacy and empathy with someone if you actually know what they are going through—not just what you guess they're going through.

Sometimes, in the natural flow of conversation, paraphrasing, clarifying, and summarizing can be blended together. The trick is to maintain an open, respectful, and curious attitude to the other person, and don't make assumptions—you may be surprised at what you learn when you shut up and pay attention!

Active listening doesn't have to be fancy or complicated.

To **paraphrase**, literally repeat what they've said using synonyms. If they say, "I could sleep for a week," you could say, "Poor you, you sound tired!"

To **clarify**, you could literally take the same observation and frame it as a question. "Would you say you're exhausted right now?"

To **summarize**, all you have to do is find the nub of what they're communicating. Here, a good trick is to ask what the overall *emotional* message is. They may never literally say, "I'm tired," but if they give you a five-minute list of everything they've had to do that day and tell you about the four cups of coffee they've had just to keep awake, then you are summarizing when you say, "Wow. So all in all, you're running on empty right now?"

Notice that this last sentence is, in a way, a paraphrase, a clarifying question, and a summary all in one. That's because when we clarify, we are not just looking to gather accurate information; we're also demonstrating our willingness to listen, our interest, and our reassurance that we care enough to get the details right. Similarly, a summary or paraphrase isn't there to add information or solve a problem—it's primarily there to signal, "I'm listening. I heard you." Here are some other turns of phrase you can use:

If I've understood you correctly, you're saying that...?

So XYZ... is that right?

Did I understand you when you said that...?

It seems like...

Wait, could you tell me more about...?

When did this start/what happened next/what do you think about this?

I'm not sure I understand. Could you explain what you mean when you say...

Takeaways

- No matter who you are, it's always possible to improve your people skills and become a more charming and more likeable conversationalist.
- Start by building more social awareness. If eye contact is often awkward or uncomfortable, try the triangle technique: Draw an imaginary inverted triangle on the other person's face around their eyes and mouth. During the conversation, change your gaze every five to ten seconds.
- Be aware of proxemics as a nonverbal mode of communication. Intimate, social, personal or public space are used in different contexts and can signal intentions, with people regulating their social closeness by changing their physical proximity.
- "Perceptual positions" can help you build empathy and switch perspectives. First position is seeing the world through our eyes, second position is seeing the world through someone else's eyes, and third position is seeing the world through a neutral observer's eyes. You can gain insight into a situation by adopting each position in turn.

- To be a better and more active listener, paraphrase, clarify and summarize. Avoid judging, interpreting through your own perspective or interrupting, and simply listen.

Chapter 2: The Power of Empathy

A Truly Genuine Compliment

Many people say that flattery will get you nowhere in life. Are they right?

Well, it may be that the *right* compliment can actually work magic. You can probably think of a time when someone paid you a compliment that completely made your day, not only making you feel like a million bucks, but also changing the way you viewed the person giving the compliment.

Lindsay Liben is a psychotherapist and clinical social worker who sees genuine compliments as little nuggets of goodwill that strengthen connections. "**Compliments can be a useful tool to nurture and enhance relationships. Ultimately it contributes to deeper, more intimate connection**," she says. Compliments make everyone feel good—you included—and they help foster feelings of warmth and rapport.

But, they have to be done the right way! Here's how.

Tip 1: make it authentic

Think about something you admire, respect, or like in the other person. Choose something that relates to what you personally find valuable, or better yet, something you know speaks to *their* values.

Tip 2: make it meaningful

Why does this thing you see in them appeal to you so much? What effect does this quality have out in the world? In other words, think about the meaning of possessing this quality.

Tip 3: make it specific

Keep it simple and compliment something specific rather than going over the top and praising them to high heaven. This goes back to being authentic—ironically, the bigger the compliment, the less genuine it can feel.

People are often suspicious of flattery because it can feel shallow. This only happens when we fail to make our compliments authentic, meaningful, or specific. An example of a great compliment is, "This meal is delicious. I love how there are just so many beautiful colors in this salad!"

This would work well if you were a foodie yourself and knew that the other person cared a lot about good food. The compliment works because it's real and it means something. If someone else was at the same dinner party and glibly announced, "I think you must be the most amazing hostess in the world; your parties are legendary!" it may have come across as a little insincere. Why? Because that person doesn't especially care about being a good hostess, it's hyperbolic, and very general.

Here's where empathy comes in: you need to carefully understand what a person most values and compliment them in a way that makes them feel good in relation to that value. Do they take pride in their home? Compliment how well the lighting comes together in the living room. Have they made a big effort to look nice that day? Tell them their sweater color really makes their eyes sparkle. Do they place a lot of value on intelligence? Tell them you admire their taste in books, especially their collection of ancient Sufi poetry (provided this is true, of course!).

Sometimes, people warn against complimenting superficial things, like appearances. But this is perfectly fine if done right. Try to link it back to a quality you know is important for that person, i.e., compliment their good taste or how well an item flatters them. Try to compliment things that people *do* rather than things they *are*, i.e., "I love that you're always smiling so much!" will feel better than, "You're pretty." Likewise, "Nice work," is a perfectly good compliment, but why not go a step further and say something like, "Wow, you've been so thorough with this. Our whole team found your report a breeze to read!"

Finally, a few more compliment tips:

- Use the person's name (just once— too often can feel weird and uncomfortable!)
- Don't add any pressure or demands (You look amazing with your hair

down; why don't you wear it like that all the time? You totally should!)

- Compliment sparingly (once per interaction is enough)
- Under no circumstances give a compliment expressly because you expect to receive one in return
- Don't use a compliment to defuse conflict or calm down an upset person—no matter how genuine the compliment is, it will come across as insincere and even manipulative

Grasping Bids for Connection

The term "bid for connection" was first coined by therapist couple and (couples therapists!) John and Julie Gottman of the Gottman Institute (you can read about their fascinating work at Gottman.com). It's what it sounds like: a bid for attention is a person's attempt to get acceptance or affection from someone else. People, whether they're in a romantic relationship or not, have one fundamental need they are trying to satisfy when they reach out to others: connection. **When you "turn toward" bids for connection, you deepen and strengthen relationships of all kinds.**

On the one hand, as human beings we all want to feel seen, heard, and respected by the people around us. We all crave affection and warmth and to be accepted for the people we are. And yet, how many of us are really comfortable outright asking for these needs to be met? More commonly, our bids for connection end up disguised as something else.

Take a look at these behaviors:

- Telling a story about your day
- Talking loudly to catch someone's attention
- Sharing a link to a post or funny video or picture
- Initiating a hug or touching someone
- Talking about a shared interest
- Complaining or sighing repeatedly

According to the Gottmans, each of the above can actually be hidden bids for connection. Each of them may be a way for the person to say, "I want to connect. Please pay me some attention." We can respond to them in one of three ways. We can **turn toward** that bid (by connecting), we can **turn against** it (by responding with anger or upset), or we can **turn away** (by ignoring the bid completely).

Learning how to listen, to be vulnerable, and to respect someone else's vulnerability is not just for close couples. It applies to any relationship we have, whether with friends, family, or professionals. In one fascinating study, they gathered 130 newlywed couples at a retreat and observed them closely (Carrere & Gottman, 1999, "Predicting Divorce among Newlyweds from the First Three Minutes of a Marital Conflict Discussion," *Family Process*). They noticed that throughout the day, there would be bids for connection; for example, if a birdwatching enthusiast said, "Hey, look at that goldfinch!" to their partner. The comment has nothing to do with the bird, but is a request for interest, support, and connection—however small. Whether the couples turned toward, turned away, or turned against these bids was a strong predictor of whether they'd be divorced within six years. The couples who got divorced tended to turn toward bids just 30% of the time, whereas those who stayed married had done so almost ninety percent of the time.

Again, it's not just about married couples. The Gottmans noticed that the "masters" tended to scan their environment for appreciation and connection, whereas the "disasters" only scanned their environment for problems and complaints. If we want to improve our social skills and connect more with others, then we absolutely have to learn how to recognize their bids for connection and learn how to respond to them when we see them. Doing this, we build our empathy, but it's also true to say that we need a little empathy to begin with if we're going to make it work.

For starters, be aware of when people are actually making bids for connection. This isn't as mysterious as it may seem. If someone's talking to you at all, there's a good chance they're trying to start a conversation or in some basic way seek a positive response from you. One big mistake we can make is to focus just on the *content* of what's being said and not the intention. So, someone says, "Hmm, I wonder why XYZ?" and you think this idle wondering out loud doesn't really warrant any response. Or maybe you simply answer them factually, as though they were looking for the literal answer to that question. Either way, the conversation shuts down and the other person doesn't get the connection they were surreptitiously asking for.

Here are a few more examples:

Bid: "Oh man, have I had the longest day today. You wouldn't believe it . . ."

Turn against: "*You've* had a long day? Sitting on the couch?

Turn away: "Cool."

Turn toward: "Yeah? What happened?"

Bid: "Haha, look at this guy in the paper!"

Turn against: "Shh, I'm watching my show!"

Turn away: (nods without looking at the story in the paper)

Turn toward: "Here, let me see . . ."

Of course, not everything a person does is a bid for connection. Another caveat is that "connection" might look like different things for different people. But it's not that complicated—you don't have to do very much but "turn toward." That can be as simple as communicating to the person, "Yes? I'm here and I'm listening. What's going on with you?" Sometimes, you can communicate enormous amounts of

45

validation and attention by literally turning your body to face someone and showing them that you're giving them your full attention.,

Human beings tend to have an unspoken but silly rule: you are not allowed to explicitly and deliberately ask for interaction, affection, validation, or attention. So we talk in circles around it, pretending to ask for something else, and then find ourselves in confusion or conflict when we get what we didn't want!

How can you use this insight to make your own interactions go more smoothly and reach genuine connection with others more quickly? Firstly, pay attention to how people are behaving. Don't look only at the *words* they're saying, but a little deeper to try to understand the *intention* behind those words. Could they be asking for attention, affection (yes, even friends and colleagues can want their version of affection!), validation, reassurance, or just plain to connect with you?

It can be hard to see sometimes, especially if someone's bids are to complain, find fault, or sigh passively aggressively until you ask them what's wrong. But the great thing about bids for connection is that when connection is made, they disappear. When people feel you responding to their need for connection (even, perhaps, a connection they themselves are not aware of!), then you will automatically feel more empathetic to them and your relationships will thrive.

The Art of Nonviolent Communication

One of the most useful frameworks you may ever use in social situations is called non-violent communication, or NVC. First created by mediator and communications coach Marshal Rosenberg, the theory is about honest, effective, and empathic communication that will completely change the way you engage with others—whether that's on a deep personal level or simply with colleagues and acquaintances (*Nonviolent Communication—A Language of Life: Life-Changing Tools for Healthy Relationships*, 2015)

The "violence" in this model encompasses verbal aggression, veiled threats, manipulation, force, criticism, judgment, or even excessive praise (which is, after all, a kind of judgment!). Non-violent communication, then, is communication free from these things, in which all parties feel heard, respected, and understood.

Rosenberg was a prolific writer, but his framework can be broken down into four simple steps:

Step 1: Observe without judgment

Saying, "You're late to the dinner we arranged," is an observation.

Saying, "Why can't you do a simple thing like show up on time?" is a judgment.

Step 2: Express your feelings

Expressing feelings is often an overlooked part of communication, sometimes because we simply assume that it's obvious or that other people should be able to guess. Again, try to express how you feel without judgment, without blame, and without dragging the other person into it in any way. You could say, "I'm feeling unimportant and overlooked."

Be careful here. Sometimes we think we're expressing how we feel when we're actually lobbing grenades at the other person. Saying, "You make me feel unappreciated," or, "I'm angry at your disrespect," is actually making a claim about the other person (they are being disrespectful) or blaming them for the way that you feel. No prizes for guessing how the other person will respond if you approach things like this!

Instead, just stick to saying how you feel, and keep it simple. Avoid "you make me feel . . ." Just become aware of yourself and the emotion you're feeling without attaching an interpretation, theory, or judgment to it.

Step 3: Express your needs

This one is important. According to Rosenberg, the whole point of communication is to get our needs met. Again, you want to frame this in a non-violent way, i.e., without judgment or threat or force. Obviously, saying, "I need for you to not be a stupid idiot," is not exactly a legitimate need! Try not to frame your needs as something the other person is compelled to take responsibility for.

For example, say, "I have a need to feel appreciated and loved." Short and sweet. Avoid saying something like, "You need to be better." Your needs should be expressed neutrally and without reference to any person, in the same way as you would say, "I need air," or "I need to eat to survive."

Step 4: Express specific requests

Too many people jump in at this step without covering the previous three. Your requests should be based on and flow directly from your feelings and your needs. For example, if you are feeling unimportant and that your need for appreciation and love is not getting met, then the request you would make is a natural extension from this: you would ask that the other person does something that helps you feel more appreciated and important.

But you need to be specific. Instead of saying, "I'm asking you to appreciate me more," say, "I'm asking that you show up on time so I can feel like you appreciate me."

And then, you stop speaking. No psychological games, no blaming or guilt-tripping, no aggression (or passive aggression), and no good guy versus bad guy. You simply claim your own needs and own your own feelings, and in expressing these, make *reasonable requests* of the other person. Importantly, they are just that: requests. Just because you've communicated non-violently, it doesn't mean the other person must comply with that request. Once you're done talking, it's time to listen to the other person. They, too, get to express their observations, their feelings, their needs, and their requests of you.

The NVC model is a brilliant way to defuse conflict and make breakthrough connections when people are feeling hurt or misunderstood. It's also a very good way to improve your everyday conversations, though, and will help you make a subtle shift in how you interact with everyone you meet. It's all about tone and intention.

The thing is, all human beings have needs, and in fact, we all share the same universal needs to be heard, respected, and valued for the individuals we are. Conflict happens whenever people feel like these needs are not being met. So, if you approach any conflict or conversation with the intention to express your own needs and respect those of the other person, almost all conflict disappears and real connection can take its place. Here are a few more things to keep in mind as you practice this shift in mindset:

- Remember that the purpose of communication is not to win but to connect
- Always start with an observation, which you can combine with listening

("It seems like . . ."), which will slow things down and signal to the other person that you are actually listening and present, rather than gearing up to fight your own agenda.

- Talk about your feelings and not the issues. People can waste so much time debating details when what instantly creates connections is talking about how they feel about those details

- Be ultra-careful about making other people responsible for your feelings. If you say you feel "hurt" or "misunderstood," for example, you are implying the other person is hurting you, or that they don't understand you. It can feel really hard to rephrase your emotions so that they don't do this.

- Describe rather than judge or interpret. Your initial goal is to just express where you are and understand where the other person is. Sometimes people go into amateur therapist mode and want to elaborate on a grand theory about why things are as they are—avoid this and just state what is going on from your perspective.

Realistically, such a formal way of engaging can be cumbersome and unnatural for people, and those you encounter casually are going to find it weird if you suddenly start talking this way! But, outside of serious conflict, there is one very clever way to use Rosenberg's principles in "normal life." Every time you are communicating with someone, ask yourself what their unmet need is and *then talk directly to that.*

Rosenberg gives an example of a bald teacher insulting and criticizing a male student's overly long hair. There are many ways to interpret and respond to this, but if you think in terms of need, you'll probably see that the bald teacher feels insecure about his baldness and is putting the student down to feel better about himself. His unmet need is to feel valued and appreciated for who he is, and his words convey how much he doesn't feel that.

Whether you use this approach to dissolve more serious conflict in your close relationships, or simply use it to gain deeper insight into the motivations of the people you encounter more casually, thinking in terms of needs and feelings is a powerful way to bring more empathy into your relationships.

It also helps you take responsibility for your own emotions and reactions. If you combine this model with, for example, perspective-switching as described above, you may discover just how your own unmet needs and the unmet needs of others are affecting the way you communicate. Try it the next time you communicate with anyone for any reason: **as you talk, quickly check in and ask—what are my needs here, and what are theirs?** Then use observation, expression of feelings and needs, and reasonable requests to help get *both* your needs met. When it works, it's a beautiful thing.

Use Language Softeners

As the saying goes, it's not what you do, it's the way you do it. In other words, sometimes empathy in social situations is not so much what you're saying but *how* you're saying it. This is where language "softeners" come in handy—**softer language can help foster trust, empathy, and likeability in all social situations.** While most people would love to be kinder and more empathetic, the truth is, we all have a lot to learn to simply be more polite, diplomatic, and tactful!

In the 2016 book *English for Diplomatic Purposes*, Noriko Ishihara explores how varying the softness or intensity of language is a kind of "meta-cognitive strategy" that is crucial to understand when communicating, especially cross-culturally.

She explains that although speaking too aggressively, curtly, or rudely doesn't seem like that big of a deal, people are primarily emotional beings (even and especially when they don't admit it!), and the entire quality of your connection to them will be influenced by how you make them feel. Empathy is a grand goal, but in our modern world it may actually be that tact, etiquette, and politeness will get more use day to day. For example, you want to share your opinion without causing offense. You have to share upsetting news. You have to ask someone to do something they don't really want to . . .

In all these situations, it's "soft" language that will get the job done.

We can soften language in a few ways:

- Changing the pitch, tone, and volume of our voice
- Using different words and phrases

- Presenting options and suggestions rather than making demands and declarations
- Paying attention to our emphasis and intonation

Granted, what is considered polite in one culture may come across as wishy-washy in another, but for most people in most situations, a little tact generally goes a long way. Here are some strategies to use:

Use Modal Verbs

Words like could, would, and might make our requests softer and create a little distance and wiggle room. It's a way to present things to people without triggering resistance in them, keeping things in the realm of the possible rather than forcing a foregone conclusion. For example, we could say, "You could consider trying again next year when you're more prepared," or, "I might not agree with that, I'm afraid." Both of these sound way more palatable than, "Try again next year," or, "I don't agree."

Focus on the Positive

Your friend is showing you a new outfit and asking for your opinion. Saying, "It's pretty ugly," is way harsher than, "I'm not sure it's such a pretty dress." It's a subtle difference. You are no longer saying the word "ugly." Even though you are saying the dress is *not* pretty, that's still the word your friend hears. It's much gentler. Similarly, "That's stupid," is worse than saying, "I'm not sure that's the most intelligent idea you've put forward."

Use Qualifiers

Using language like "somewhat" or "a little" naturally helps soften things. When you use softeners, you are communicating to others that you are approaching the interaction with good intentions, and the matter is still open to be fixed with a little tact and diplomacy. If you've been mistakenly served a chicken soup at a restaurant when you ordered vegetarian, you could say to the waiter, "I'm sorry, but there's *a bit* of chicken in here," to soften the complaint.

Word Choice

Besides grammar, you can totally change the tone of what you're saying by choosing gentler, more polite terms. Say something is challenging rather than a problem. Say that people are having a disagreement rather than a fight. If you have to take up an issue with someone, start out by framing it as a question rather than barging in immediately with a bone to pick.

Use a Gentler Style

Use the following phrases to bring a little more tact and gentleness to what you're saying:

"I wonder . . ."
"What I'd like to know is . . ."
"Perhaps . . ."
"If I may ask, (then pose your question)."
"Can I invite you to . . ."
"Perhaps you might find this interesting."
"I'm curious about . . ."
"I'm not entirely sure, but . . ."
"What if we . . . ?"

Think of these sorts of phrases as cushions around the main idea you're trying to communicate—and cushions make people more comfortable!

However, there are some big caveats here. Being polite and tactful is not the same as being evasive, unclear, or manipulative. We are polite for one purpose only: to make other people feel more at ease, and to help create more harmonious interactions. Politeness is misused when it puts people on edge, communicates passive aggression, or creates confusion. For example, if you really do have a big problem on your hands, it won't help anyone for you to call it a "little bit of a problem."

Softened language, like the other techniques in this book, comes down to our main goal with all communication: to understand the other person and to connect with them. It's smart to use politeness and soft language if doing so eases that connection. It's not really about the words but our implied attitude of collaboration, courtesy, and civility. We can send a powerful message in *how* we speak that says, "I would like our interaction to go smoothly." Sometimes that alone can work magic.

Takeaways

- Empathy is a nonnegotiable ingredient in genuine, connected interactions, and one easy way to create it is to give compliments. Make it authentic, meaningful to the person receiving it and specific, avoiding insincere exaggeration or vague niceties that don't speak to the person's values.

- Learn to recognize "bids for attention" because when you "turn toward" these unspoken requests for connection and validation, you deepen and strengthen relationships of all kinds, and respond with empathy. Turning against or away from these requests does the opposite.
- Practice the art of nonviolent communication by using four simple steps: first, observe without judgment or interpretation. Second, express how you feel without blame or making anyone responsible. Third, express your needs plainly and assertively, without implicating the other person. Finally, calmly express a specific request that stems from the previous three steps, without entitlement or force. This will make any difficult or emotional conversation infinitely easier.
- Use language softeners. Softer language can help foster trust, empathy, and likeability in all social situations. Use modal verbs and qualifiers, focus on the positive, be mindful of your word choice and use a gentler, more respectful and unhurried style to communicate a friendly willingness to cooperate.

Chapter 3: Better Conversation Skills

Get Chunky

When it comes to people skills, arguably the most valuable is the art of conversation. Let's start with a relatively simple but underappreciated conversational technique called chunking. The term "chunking" refers to the process of arranging or breaking down information into either bigger or smaller chunks. When we apply the idea to asking questions during a conversation, **it's a strategy that may be used to vary the level of information you get coming back to you. This way, you can reach an agreement, acquire more and correct detail, or even persuade people to move from one plane of thought to another**. Ultimately, it makes you a better—and more masterful—conversationalist.

George A Miller was a Harvard psychologist who fleshed out this theory in the 1950s. His big insight was into the way the human brain processes information. There are natural limits that we need to work around—too much detail is a problem, but so is too little ("The Magical Number Seven, Plus or Minus Two: Some Limits on our Capacity for Processing Information," 1956). We can work around these limits, however, with chunking.

Let's begin with "chunking down" where we use questions to bring the other person down to a less abstract, more detailed level. For example, you might be chatting to someone who is excitedly telling you their big visions and dreams, but you ask them something like, "So what do you think the next step is?" or, "What do you think is fundamentally causing this problem in the first place?"

Chunking down questions is about finding out more and filling in the gaps of your understanding. It's about detail, as though you were zooming in with a microscope. But if you zoom in too closely, you lose the bigger picture, so to speak! Enter "chunking down" or asking questions that seek to understand the bigger picture that all the details come together to form. So, someone might tell you twenty little details about problems they're having with a project, and you could say, "What do you think all these problems indicate?" or, "What are you actually trying to achieve with this project?" This is like zooming out again and reminding yourself of the bigger picture.

Chunking up and down, then, are just like varying the degree of specificity versus generality. Your questions are a way to turn the dial on the microscope to zoom in or out. So, if we got really good at zooming in and out at will, how would this help our conversation skills?

Well, try using chunking up to start with so you can get a broad view of what's going on. At work, for example, you can get a general outline of an issue at hand, or with a friend, you can ask very generally, "So, how's life at the moment?" When you want to identify specific goals or develop your understanding, you chunk down. For example, you pause and ask someone, "Can you tell me more?" or, "What happened next?" to gather more details.

You might need to chunk up, however, if you're looking for overall agreement. For example, after a protracted argument or negotiation, you might sit back at some point and say, "Okay, well, we disagree on a few unimportant details, sure, but we seem to have the same goal here, right?" You can also chunk up any time the problem you're trying to understand is *systematic*. So, you might have a discussion about a certain point of miscommunication with a family member, but after this happens a few times, you might like to chunk up and ask, "Why does this keep happening? What are we doing that's making us repeatedly misunderstand each other?"

Basically, we chunk up when we want to gain more general understanding or encourage it in someone else, and we chunk down when we want more detail. Chunking up allows us to explore a broader purpose or intention, or see how the smaller instance fits into the bigger whole.

Chunking down allows us to elaborate on examples, details, and explanations for a certain instance. Imagine two people disagree about what should be on the school curriculum, and things are getting heated because they're butting heads over whether religious education should have a place. One person notices they're getting bogged down in a detailed argument about the different norms and expectations around different religious orders and what they mean. To soothe this conflict, they chunk up and zoom out instead, thinking about generalized patterns, purpose, intentions, and the bigger picture.

They say, "Well, we can agree that school should be a place where children learn a wide range of social, practical, and moral lessons." The other person will almost certainly agree. You've found a source of agreement, and the argument diffuses somewhat. On the other hand, maybe you've been having a weekly counseling session where you chat pleasantly with the therapist but without really going anywhere. After thinking about it, you realize you need to chunk down, and you ask in the next session, "Do you think there is any specific, concrete thing I can be doing to help myself right now?" You zoom up and start to operate on a more generalized level where you consider bigger pictures and overall purpose.

So you can see two primary functions of chunking: chunking up can help you reach agreement, shift an argument, persuade people, or find common ground. Chunking down can help a wishy-washy process become clearer and more focused, or help you narrow in on actions rather than just getting lost in theory.

We can chunk up *and* down in conversations. Imagine we are using a funnel. We could start at the wide end and move to the narrow end of the funnel, or vice versa. At the wide end, we ask open-ended questions (those that can have any answer; for example, "What do you think of XYZ?"), and at the narrow end, we ask more closed questions (those that have only a specific or yes/no answer; for example, "What's your name?" or, "Have you seen this movie?").

If you're getting to know someone more deeply, you can move from general to more specific (i.e., a "probing" style). They say they love films; you ask about their favorite film. They tell you *Casablanca*, and you ask about what they loved most about it, and so on. Depending on the context, this could be an inquisition-style interview or a fascinating getting-to-know-you conversation! This kind of funnel also allows you to zoom in on a specific problem or solution and, in the process, help calm people down and defuse tension. "Can you tell me what specifically has upset you?"

General-to-specific funnels are great for putting people at ease and gradually working your way to asking more personal questions. You watch closely and ramp up the specificity of your questions as time goes on:

Step 1: Ask a general, open-ended question ("So what are you planning for the Christmas holidays?").

Step 2: Ask for a general explanation that builds on their answer ("Oh, that sounds fun. Do you have a big family?").

Step 3: Go in for detail ("I have a brother too! He drives me nuts. What about yours? Do you guys get on well?").

Step 4: Go for the finest possible detail ("Wait, can you tell me his name again? I think I knew him. Did he graduate XYZ High in 1992?").

From the narrowest point of the funnel, you can open up questions again. In conversation, try to follow the basic rules:

- Move from the general to specific, and always start with a general question.

- Vary your questions to gain more insight, and don't stay too long at any one level.
- Pay close attention to your conversation partner's response. If they are finding detailed questions uncomfortable, irrelevant, or difficult to answer, try to zoom out and come in again more gradually; likewise, notice if someone is frustrated with a too-general level of questioning and try to be more focused.

If you're ever in a conversation that feels either like it's heading toward conflict or is fizzling out in boredom or misunderstanding, quickly check in and ask 1) what level of detail is the conversation at and 2) are we both on the *same* level? Then adjust accordingly.

Use Clean Language

In your daily conversations, you may encounter someone who expresses themselves better using metaphors. **To better understand and connect with that person, try to use what's called "clean language." This is a questioning technique used for discovering,**

exploring, and working with people's metaphors without contaminating them.

The approach was originally developed by psychotherapist David Grove in the 1980s, who wanted to develop a technique for more effective communication. When exploring the styles of the most successful therapists, he found they all had a way of adopting their clients' "frame of reference" as their own (Grove, et. al., *Resolving Traumatic Memories: Metaphors and Symbols in Psychotherapy*, 1989).

According to Grove, when you speak in clean language, you're holding up a mirror to others, reflecting their own words, gestures, and voice. This makes you connect better with them, cut down on misunderstandings, and create feelings of empathy and understanding.

Here are a few possible clean language questions:

And is there anything else about . . .?

And what kind of . . . is that . . .?

And where is . . .?

And whereabouts?

And what happens next?

And then what happens?

And what happens just before . . .?

And where does/could . . . come from?

And that's . . . like what?

To apply clean language in your conversations, first, **you must listen to metaphors.** When speaking with someone, pay close attention to what he or she says. Your objective is to figure out what metaphors he or she uses to describe their experiences.

Second, **speak slowly and mimic the person you're talking to.** When the person has finished speaking, you can clarify what they said by asking one of the nine clean language questions above. With each clean language question you ask, your conversation partner is likely to gain new insights, as are you. Continue asking questions until they've fully explored their emotions and potentially found a solution to their problem.

Some examples will make this idea clearer. Person A may say, "I'm feeling stuck in the mud with this whole thing," and Person B responds by saying, "We'll get you over the hurdle, don't worry." It may seem like a small thing, but the metaphors here are not consistent—the original metaphor has been "contaminated." If Person B had instead said, "Tell me more about what you think is keeping you stuck right now," then they would have been using clean language.

Using clean language, you can ask questions that ask the other person to develop their metaphor ("What kind of thing is X?"), understand the cause and effect, ("What happened just before?") or epxlore intention and purpose ("Why did X happen?").

Step 1: Just listen
Have your ears pricked (there's a metaphor!) for any metaphors they're using. For example, "I'm battling this guy at work," or, "We're speaking different languages").

Step 2: Ask questions
Staying within the same metaphor, ask questions (here, your questions can chunk up or chunk down, to combine techniques). For example, "So what's the big fight really about?" or, "What language is he speaking, and what language are you speaking?" A

good tip is to speak much more slowly and carefully as you respond.

Step 3: Continue the conversation
The metaphor may be set aside as the conversation continues, and if so, simply listen out for any new ones that are introduced. Continue to keep in mind how the person is conceptualizing the issue; for example, remember that they frame the problem as a war/battle rather than a competition or game—this alters how you speak as the conversation unfolds.

Clean language is really an exercise is empathy, and if you try it, you'll instantly notice that it's easier to get on the same wavelength as other people. This will make them feel more heard by you, and it will also help you better understand what they're experiencing, and the issue in general. Just remember to keep your ego out of things and try not to assume what people mean. Really believe what they're telling you and talk to them where they are, rather than from your interpretation. The interesting thing about this technique is that the other person may never actually be aware that you're using it—but they will feel that you are more attentive, more empathetic, and that you "get" them!

Being good at conversations and developing social skills is about being creative and flexible with the way you communicate. You need to be neutral, non-directed, and unbiased—which essentially means not influencing or twisting the information you're being given by the other person. If you've ever been accused of "not listening" to people, then it's likely you *were* listening, but you were just hearing what you wanted to hear! It's human to make assumptions, to predict, to guess, or just to fill in the blanks with what people tell us, but this can also mean that we're susceptible to missing the nuance and meaning of what people really want to share with us. In other words, we are inside our own metaphors and not really grasping other peoples'.

If we use clean language, though, we gain clarity and insight, break down barriers, and better understand one another, while cutting down on misunderstanding. Here are a few things to keep in mind:

- Don't interrupt. Pause a little after they speak to show you're digesting what they've said and want them to fully express everything they want to say.

- Try to forget about your "world" and immerse instead in theirs. How does the situation look from their point of view regardless of your own?
- Literally mimic them. For example, if they keep saying "hostage" or keep returning to a metaphor of being lost in the woods, then imagine yourself copying and pasting those exact terms and phrases and using them yourself.
- Also paraphrase them. If they elaborate on a metaphor of being lost in the woods, you can echo this by talking about wandering aimless, or not being able to see the way out.

Clean language is always useful, whether you're trying to show empathy or gently persuade someone to your point of view. The irony is that you can usually best persuade someone when you *first* understand their point of view! When you are willing and unable to completely understand and step into someone else's worldview, then you are both much more likely to find a harmonious connection together.

Use the Improv Technique "HPM" to Get Through Awkward Conversations

Chunking and clean language are not the only clever ways to navigate conversations. One very simple technique actually comes from the world of improv comedy, where thinking on your feet is essential. **One of the most effective improv comedy techniques is called HPM, which stands for History, Philosophy, and Metaphor. Use this technique and you will never run out of things to say in a conversation again.**

First, to explore the history angle, you can mention a *personal* past experience relating to the topic. Next, for the philosophical angle, you can demonstrate what you feel or think regarding something, or your general "philosophy" on a particular topic. And lastly, close it with the metaphor angle by adding metaphors or figures of speech (remembering the power of metaphors from the last section, you can see that this also in effect invites other people to take a peek into your worldview and perspective).

The HPM framework is like having a "mental template" that you may use in both good and terrible times. It's a concept that can be applied to any topic at any time, and best of all, it makes no difference how smart or creative you or the people you're talking to are! When you run out of things to say, you can always rely on HPM to add some flavor to your conversation. If you notice a conversation is feeling awkward, stalled, or a little weird, just remember this simple acronym and it will come to your rescue.

For example, when you're talking to someone about bands or music, you can apply HPM this way:

History (mention a past experience): "Late 2016, I saw Grimes at Glastonbury!"

Philosophy (demonstrate what you feel): "I was so amazed with her performance! It was a great experience for me and my friends!"

Metaphor (describe it in metaphor): "Grimes is like a musical space fairy. Her sound makes me feel like I'm floating on the galaxy!"

Here's another example:

You're casually chatting to someone new in your exercise class and things are a little stilted because you don't really know them and on the surface don't appear to have much in common. They mention it's their first class, and you spot a chance to squeeze in an HPM: "Oh, I remember *my* first class. It was excruciating! I started out thinking it would be too easy, but after about twenty minutes in, I was seeing my life flash before my eyes . . . at the end of the class, they basically had to scrape me off the floor."

Use this technique and you will never run out of things to say in a conversation again. Though asking questions to get over a lull in the conversation can work wonders, sometimes you can ask too many questions, and the other person will feel a little like they're being interviewed. Instead, make an HPM statement and watch how the conversation starts flowing again.

A great way to start an HPM observation is with: "This reminds me of . . ." and then you can connect it with literally anything that is happening around you. It's also a great save when you're talking to a reserved or unresponsive person who isn't really running with the questions you're asking. As you can imagine, you can mix things up a bit with this technique, adding a little more H here or a lot more M there. Or you could combine them all together for something that's a more casual and spontaneous blend. The more you practice, the more you'll get the hang of it!

The HPM technique works because it subtly reframes the goals of the conversation. Too many people get trapped in awkward conversations because they're too worried about appearing smart or interesting or proving something. Bur borrowing from the world of improv reframes the goal to something else: fun. By using HPM, you are revealing a little about yourself and keeping the flow of the conversation going. You touch on universally appealing subjects that people will be able to connect with—and you do it all without needing to be witty or super intelligent!

A few tips:

- Be relaxed and confident about it. Don't try too hard to be funny or interesting.
- Keep it short and sweet.
- *Don't* try to rehearse an HPM. The technique works best when it's spontaneous and in response to something you've been told or seen as the conversation unfolds.

- Don't be afraid to show a little of yourself. Relate histories, opinions, and metaphors that speak to your values and how you want other people to see you.

Just recall an event from your past, state how it made you feel, and then add in a metaphor for a little color. This can be done easily, even in one sentence! Or you could draw it out and take longer to deliver your HPM, allowing the other person to step in and make observations or ask you questions:

"It's my first class."
"Oh God, I remember *my* first class!"
"Yeah? What was that like?"
"Well . . . I started out thinking it would be too easy, but after about twenty minutes in, I was seeing my life flash before my eyes."
"Haha! Sounds like me. Well, now you've gone and made me feel a lot more nervous."
"Well, what can I say, at the end of the class, they basically had to scrape me off the floor."
"*Really*?!"
"Yup. But that was like three months ago. I'm much stronger now."
"I see. So you started out at this gym just three months ago?"

"Well, no, actually, I've been signed up here for a few years, but blah blah blah . . ."

Use Markers to Tell Your Listener Where the Conversation is Going

When talking to someone, it's important that you both know where your conversation is headed. There are two such conversational markers we can learn to use to improve our social skills:

1) signposting
2) transitional words/sentences

Both techniques simply make conversations smoother and cohesive. They give the listener an indication of where communication is actually going. If people know why they're having a conversation and what direction it's going, they process faster and have a better idea of what to expect. This means a lot more ease and harmony for all involved! If you've ever felt trapped in a rambly, pointless conversation where you started wondering, "When is this ever going to end?" or, "What's the point of this conversation, anyway?" then you've been the victim of a conversation that lacks signposting and transition words!

SIGNPOSTS

Small words and phrases like "well, actually, as a matter of fact, etc." placed at the beginning of a sentence give the listener a good indication of what they are about to hear. These indicators serve as "warnings," allowing the listener to anticipate what is to come. They give the listener an idea if you're going to shift to another point of view, so they can cognitively prepare. The conversation feels more fluent and easier than if you had just blurted out something that was in direct contradiction without any warning.

Signposts that say "I'm about to disagree or change direction" are:

Well, frankly
Actually
As a matter of fact
I'm sorry, but

Even though they're tiny, these little words help calm and smooth the interaction. Without them, conversations can feel chopped up, abrupt, or even rude. For example, if you say, "It's probably going to rain tomorrow," and I immediately say, "The forecast predicted sun," it sounds rude, disjointed, and even a little hostile. Far better for me to say, "*Actually*, I believe the weather report I read said there was sun!" I'm still disagreeing and taking the conversation somewhere else, but I'm not allowing that disagreement to derail the conversation or make things feel awkward.

Instead, signposts allow you to build smooth connections between ideas and clearly signal to the listener when you are about to take a turn. We keep our listener's attention and present information to them rather than just dumping data in their laps and expecting them to make sense of it!

Another example of a signpost is when people say something like, "There were three main issues here; first . . ." This signals to the listener that there will be three things listed in order. It's a courtesy and prevents the listener from feeling like they're left hanging as you go through your list, which could be any length as far as they know. Another example is when you say, "Okay, I have good news and bad news. The good news is . . ." You are giving the listener a few moments to prepare for the fact they are about to hear something that might be unpleasant.

Here are a few more types of signposts that can help you navigate tricky conversations:

"Emotions ahead" – You're about to share feelings, some of which may be difficult. "I want to be really honest with you here . . ." or, "I'm feeling (pause) XYZ."

"Awkward alert" – You're aware something is uncomfortable. "I don't know how to say this," or, "This is a little embarrassing, but . . ."

"Bad news coming" – Warning your listener to prepare for disappointment. "I wish I didn't have to say this, but . . ." or, "I'm really sorry it's come to this. However . . ."

These sorts of signposts can seem almost too obvious and simple, but they do make a difference. They hold up a metaphorical sign for your listener, easing conversation, but they also communicate a little bit of tact, respect, and self-awareness that will help you create more harmony and understanding.

TRANSITIONS

Smoothly moving from one idea to the next using transitions is not just for written language but spoken, too. Transitions are there to help you structure your speech in a logical, flowing way as a courtesy for the person listening. It makes you come across as more likeable, trustworthy, in control, and empathetic.

Example transitions are:

And, even more, further, moreover, too, in the second place (all about **addition**)

And then, afterward, meanwhile, at the same time, subsequently, whenever, this time round (all about **time** and sequence of events)

To demonstrate, for instance, as an example (to **exemplify** or show examples)

But, however, likewise, in the same way, similarly, in contrast, to put it another way, nonetheless, after all (to **compare and contrast**)

That's why, so, since, because, and for that reason, therefore, as a result (cause and effect **explanation**)

You have to understand, to clarify, to rephrase, that is to say (to help **clarify** your point)

Of course, without doubt, surely, in fact, to repeat (**intensification** of your point)

Granted, I can see that, to be sure (**concession** to their point)

In sum, to conclude, in the end, that's a long way of saying, ultimately, in brief, to finish up (**summarizing**)

While signposts help signal to your listener that you're about to take a subtle change in the conversational direction, transitions are there to link and smooth things over (in fact, did you spot the transition in the previous sentence, and the transition in *this* one? Read these two sentences again without the transitions and see what gets lost).

Transitions and signposts can be used incorrectly, though. Be careful about putting them in just for the sake of it, or else it will come across as unnatural. They should make things flow more and be clearer and more logical—if they don't, they should be abandoned. Be careful to use signposts and transitions as they are intended. For example, if you're a person who consistently premises their *opinions* with "in fact," you are going to annoy and confuse your listeners! If you keep saying "actually" and then proceed not to correct the person but basically repeat what they've just said, you're misusing transitions. Finally, watch out for overuse. Too many can make your speech seem more awkward not less, especially if you're overusing the more formal expressions like "therefore" and "furthermore."

One extra tip is to watch your nonverbal expression as you use transitions and signposts to let your listener know where the conversation is going. You can also signal a shift in tone or a change in topic by sitting back in your seat, leaning forward, lowering the pitch of your voice, taking a big obvious breath, or using hand gestures that literally signal you're making a new point. Some of us do all this naturally, but if we want to become better conversationalists overall, it's worth paying attention to **how we present information** to others, and making efforts to deliver it as smoothly and logically as possible.

Hold Conversations with Conversation Threading

Let's look at one more practical and effective conversation skill to help improve your competency with people in social settings. **Conversation threading is a method that will improve the overall quality of your engagements with others without ever feeling as if you are running out of things to say.**

It only involves four simple steps. First, to begin the conversation, ask a basic question. This gives the momentum time to grow. Second, wait for the individual to respond, then listen for conversation cues. For example, "I am a fan of **rock** music." Third, ask an open-ended inquiry on the conversation cue you just heard. This broadens the discussion. "Tell me about the last **rock** band you've seen live." Lastly, wait for the individual to respond, and then listen for cues that will allow you to ask further questions. "I enjoy this **rock** band called Charly Bliss. They aren't super famous yet, but they have some good tunes!" Then remark, followed by your open-ended inquiry, "That's incredible. Can you recommend their best **rock** song? I've been looking for new headbanger songs lately!"

Conversation threads are essentially points of interest, hooks, or leads. A thread can be an idea, a word, a phrase, anything. Usually, when we feel a conversation is boring or stuck, it's because we have tunnel vision and are no longer picking up threads and hooks to continue the conversation—but they are always there!

Using a thread, you can elaborate on certain topics and open up new avenues to other interesting conversations—a bit like the way a hyperlink on a web page takes you to another web page when clicked. Good conversations need to flow. If you stay on the same topic, it will eventually dry up and you'll be left with nothing to say. You need to consistently identify, follow, and nurture threads, offshoots, and tangents to keep the conversation alive. You can drop some threads to pick up others, returning later to old threads when you need to pep things up again.

This is an art to master, but there are also a few general rules that, if you practice, will make you a better conversationalist in time. Imagine that all the threads are literally the fabric of the conversation, holding it all together. But how do you consciously create and use these threads?

Person A, for example, says, "How was your holiday?" and Person B says, "It was great! It rained on the last day, but we went on some awesome hikes. We flew back yesterday."

Pausing for a second, we can see that there are actually several conversational threads we could potentially pick up here: rain, hiking, air travel. When you grab ahold of any of these, you are creating a thread; for example, you can latch on to "hiking" and run with it.

"Oh wow, were these really long and grueling hikes?"

"Where did you go hiking?"

"Did your whole family hike with you?"

Depending on how the person responds to each of these above questions, they generate yet more threads. You can follow the hiking thread for a few minutes and see where it takes you. As you go, you are generating more and more topics of potential interest to pursue. You listen carefully and grab hold of what interests you, or what seems to inspire the most passion in the other person. The more threads, the more you're able to actually ignore the threads that aren't interesting to you or which you don't want to pursue. This is more useful than you realize since it gives you an out of a potentially boring tangent!

Perhaps the word you home in on is in fact "awesome" and you decide to follow this thread by asking for more details about the awesomeness of the hikes. "So, what was the best part of the hike?" or "Let me ask you, if I wanted to go on the single best hike in that area, which one should I choose?" The great thing about listening out for *emotional* threads is that you quickly build rapport and energy by amplifying what the other person is putting out emotionally. Obviously, you don't want to amplify unhappy or angry feelings, but reflecting on the speaker's excitement or interest is a guaranteed way to get a conversation going.

One more point: to be a better conversationalist, it's worth paying attention to what you say and whether you're giving your conversation partner enough hooks or threads to work with. If you routinely reply in single syllables or answer open-ended questions with "yup," then you're making it hard for the other person, who might not be willing to do the work for too long.

Here are a few more tricks to keep in mind as you master the art of threading together fascinating and worthwhile conversations:

- As before, drop your ego and don't try to force the conversation anywhere, but be loose and let it emerge in the moment. Preconceived ideas create force, and this stops the flow and the connection.
- Always pay attention to the other person and be mindful of their interest levels. You can choose which threads to follow, but also notice which threads seem most interesting to your conversation partner and pursue those. If a thread seems to be running out of steam (one-word answers, dropping interest), then let it go and pick up something else.
- If someone has taken the risk of revealing something quite outlandish, emotional, or unexpected, pick that as your thread! Assume that if someone mentions it, it's up for conversation.
- If you're really struggling, ask an open-ended question. In the answer you get, you may find another hook or thread to grab hold of.

- Prioritize emotional content and look for shared experience to create rapport and a feeling of bonding. "Oh, so you hike? Me too! Not when the weather's like this, though . . ."

To recap, the process is simple: ask a question, listen for an interesting hook, and then ask a further question about that. This technique can be nicely combined with the techniques described above—start with a general question and funnel down to a specific one as you follow a thread, and play with chunking up or down as you go. Blend in some of your own stories with an HPM—which is also a great way to abandon a thread that's gone bad! Overall, good conversationalists use a *combination* of clean language, conversational markers and transitions, and flowing threads to connect with others. In time, with practice, you too can learn to blend these approaches and become someone who is well-liked, approachable, and super fun to talk to.

Takeaways:

- One useful conversational skill is chunking, where you vary the level of information you get coming back to you. This way, you can reach an agreement, acquire more and correct detail, or even persuade people to move from one plane of thought to another. Chunk up to gain a broader view everyone can agree on, and chunk down to find detail. Move from general to specific, keeping the other person's reactions in mind.

- Use clean language to discover, explore and work with people's metaphors without "contaminating" them. Listen for metaphors used, ask questions about them and continue the conversation using the same language and imagery to show your understanding.

- Use the HPM technique to always have something to say in conversations. Talk about history (a past experience) philosophy (your feelings on it) and a metaphor (describe both with a vivid metaphor). Keep is short, sweet and natural.

- Use signposting and transitional words to tell your listeners where your story is going. Signal what is coming and link your ideas logically using words that guide your listener's understanding.

- Use conversational threading. Listen out for emotional hooks and pursue the conversation in that direction. Follow the most exciting or interesting leads and return to old, unexplored ones when conversation flags or ideas run out.

Chapter 4: Navigating Boundaries

Understanding Basic Assertiveness Techniques

With heightened social awareness of yourself and others (chapter 1), stronger empathy (chapter 2), and a few smart tricks to create a fun, flowing conversation (chapter 3), you're well on your way to being one of those warm, likeable, and sociable people we all love to be around. But obviously, conversations aren't all rainbows and buttercups, and **there will be times when you need to assert your own needs and rights firmly, but without encroaching on the needs and rights of others.**

We've already hinted at tact and politeness in earlier chapters, but assertiveness is a step further than this. According to Australia's Center for Clinical Interventions module *Assert Yourself!* (Michel, 2008*)*, assertiveness is a balanced response that is neither passive nor aggressive, and it relies heavily on self-confidence. An assertive person treats others as equals and strives to be transparent about their desires, opinions, and feelings. To practice assertiveness, here are a few basic but very effective practical techniques. Use them when you're dealing with a difficult or pushy person, or in situations where you need to say no:

Stuck Record Technique

If the other person keeps questioning, arguing, or pushing at a boundary, try simply repeating what you want again and again without becoming upset, angry, or sidetracked. If someone keeps deflecting or avoiding a question, keep repeating it to avoid getting carried away in distracting debate and pointless detail. The trick is to remain calm, be extremely specific about what you want, keep on track, and don't give up!

"Could you cover for me on Friday again?" (Said by someone who has been repeatedly taking advantage of your kindness)
"I'm sorry, I can't do it!"

"Oh, come on . . . just this once?"
"I'm really sorry, but no, I can't do it."
"Jeez. What am I supposed to do now? There's nobody else to cover but you."
"Yeah, sorry. I just can't do it, though."

The Positive No

This technique lets you communicate to the asker (and to yourself) that you're declining because you have good priorities that you're working on and saying yes to, and that you don't have the time or capacity to take on another commitment. We all want to be polite and maintain social harmony, so saying no while keeping things positive is a must.

"I'm sorry, but I'm spending time with my family that weekend."
"Thank you for the invite, but I've had a long week and need some down time at the moment."

Sometimes, assertiveness is needed not to turn down people's requests, but to put up a kind of shield when you're being attacked, intruded on, or criticized. Whether the complaint is legitimate or not, the *way* that people attack can mean you need to put up your shields and artfully deflect their negativity.

Negative Inquiry

This is an interesting skill in which we encourage the other person to be more assertive by purposely triggering their criticism. You're essentially seeking for clarification on specific statements made about you. These statements could be accusatory or critical in nature. The other person might not even notice you're controlling the discussion if you use this skill. For example, a person says, *"The meal you cooked was awful!"* but instead of going on the defensive and denying it or attacking them, you can respond with, *"What is it about the meal that didn't taste good?"*

This may seem counterintuitive, but it actually gives you the upper hand and makes you come across as more confident and in control. Suddenly, *you* are steering the conversation because you are asking questions and directing the topics that are discussed.

Negative Assertion

Using this technique, you accept your flaws and shortcomings by summarizing the criticism of those flaws and mistakes. This assertiveness skill helps you to maintain a calm demeanor in the face of criticism or complaint without getting overly defensive or unduly defending your actions. For instance, if the other person confronts you with something, you could respond by saying, *"Yeah, I can be really rude sometimes. I should really be more aware of that."* You are basically communicating "tell me something I don't know" and signaling the fact that you are not and will not be flustered by criticism! It can really take the wind out of the complainer's sails, because you already know what they're saying, so there's little point for them to continue criticizing.

When you practice any of these techniques, try to remember your nonverbal communication, too. Stand up straight and speak clearly and simply. Remember "soft language"? When it comes to being more assertive, you want to actually downplay the softness of your language and err more on the side of being direct and clear rather than conciliatory.

When establishing a boundary, saying no, accepting blame, or apologizing, you need to keep it **short, clear, and sincere**. Don't keep repeating yourself or change what you say. If you're putting up a boundary, don't weaken it by apologizing or making concessions. Depending on the situation, you can maintain politeness by simply smiling, using a warm or neutral tone of voice, and adopting a calm demeanor. If *you* really believe what you're saying, it's so much easier for others to.

Use the DESC Model for Assertive Communication

When you're assertive, you can stand up for your rights and at the same time respect others' thoughts, beliefs, and feelings. But sometimes, people lack assertiveness because they are worried about offending others, hurting them, or stepping on their toes. The DESC model was outlined by Sharon and Gordon Bower in their 2004 book, *Asserting Yourself*. It's an approach that allows you to be assertive without arousing defensiveness in other people. This will make it much easier to maintain strong, healthy boundaries, which in turn will help with navigating difficult conversations effectively.

The acronym stands for:

Describe the Situation—describe the behavior that is affecting you in a negative way, but stick only to the facts.

Express the emotion or effect—how you are being affected, using "I statements" that don't assign blame.

Solution—suggest a specific outcome that would resolve the issue.

Conclusion/consequences—what will happen if the behavior is changed and what will happen if it isn't.

Applying DESC in conversation sounds a little something like this:

(D) "Harry, I still have lots of pending tasks, and you're giving me another task with a tight deadline at very short notice. **(E)** I feel so pressured and overwhelmed because I don't know which one to prioritize. For the new task to be done, I would need some adjustments. **(S)** I hope we could set a meeting and talk about the re-prioritization of the tasks so I can manage my time effectively. **(C)** This way, I could work productively and deliver great results on time."

The idea with a statement such as the one above is that it asserts a boundary, expresses needs and emotions, and makes clear a way forward, all without raising any hackles or encouraging defensiveness in the listener. Just like with NVC, we hold our own experience with dignity and assertiveness, without being aggressive, demanding, or disrespectful of the other person's experience.

Communication so often breaks down because a balance between rights can't be found, and either we violate others' rights or feel that our own have been violated. The DESC technique is designed to find that wiggle room in between and proceed without causing these communication breakdowns. If you often feel unconfident in asking for what you want, saying no, or expressing your feelings and opinions, this technique will help.

Here's another example where the focus is more on asking for a need to be met rather than drawing a boundary:

(D) "The baby is due in just one month, and you have not booked paternity leave at work. **(E)** I feel stressed out because I'm worried we will run out of time and you won't be available to spend time with me once the baby comes. **(S)** Could you sort this out with your boss today? **(C)** This would mean I could relax knowing what our schedule will be."

The DESC model can take a little practice to work with but will help you feel focused, especially when tempers are flaring and stakes are high. A few things to remember to make this technique really work:

- Pay attention to calm, neutral body language as you speak, and make eye contact.
- Be as brief as possible. You might be tempted to keep reiterating, give examples, or explain further, but this could cause resistance in the other person, confuse things, or come across as nagging or criticism.
- If appropriate, you can take the time to write it out, or rehearse a little if you need to speak in person. You could even practice with a trusted friend or colleague to calm your nerves.

- Do your best to not get distracted by side issues, tangents, or excuses—yours or theirs. If necessary, you could use the Broken Record technique and calmly repeat what you've said.
- Finally, watch out for issuing ultimatums in the last part, the conclusion. You should outline natural consequences of behavior without making threats or being manipulative. It's better to focus on the positive outcomes of the suggested behavior rather than the negative consequences of people not complying with your request or boundary.

Learning to be assertive takes practice, but it will increase your self-esteem and resilience and, believe it or not, make others like and respect you more. The trick is that you need to genuinely feel that you are secure and confident in yourself, and not preoccupied with either pandering to others or being aggressive and dominating with them. If you can communicate this effectively, people will not feel threatened, violated, or intruded on, and so they're far more likely to actually hear what you're saying.

What do you do if people don't listen? Or worse, what do you do if people respond to your DESC statement by being hurt and defensive anyway? To be frank, this is not your problem. The beauty of being assertive is that you are conscious of your *own choice* to be respectful, neutral, and focused on harmony. If you do what you can, you know that any hurt feelings or anger from the other person are not really about you. That's simply *their choice*.

Sadly, you will encounter people who will attempt to push at boundaries in any way they can—for example, by making you feel guilty for asserting your boundary. Always remember that asserting a healthy boundary is your right (even your responsibility!) and that when done correctly, a boundary cannot cause anyone any harm. If your earnest requests are repeatedly unacknowledged and your boundaries repeatedly violated, then you always have the option of removing yourself from the situation.

Use Positive Humor Styles

According to a study by behavioral scientist Jennifer Aaker and corporate strategist Naomi Bagdonas, humor is one of the most underappreciated tools at work. They call **humor the "hidden weapon" for forging ties (as well as power, creativity, and resilience)** in their popular TED Talk, and feel we should all have more of it. But not all kinds of humor are created equal!

According to Martin et. al., the 2003 creators of the "Humor Styles Questionnaire," there are four humor styles:

Affiliative humor makes others feels better. It fosters excellent workplace interactions by encouraging interpersonal engagement, and makes social interactions of any kind warmer and more fun. People who use this type of humor are more likely to tell jokes and amusing stories, amuse others, and enjoy laughing with them. The overall effect is to make everyone feel closer, more open, and less stressed.

Example: gathered around the dinner table, you tell a hilarious story of how you encountered a ferocious Doberman on the street yesterday, but you couldn't defend yourself or run very fast because of the giant birthday cake you happened to be carrying. As you mime the ridiculous way you had to run to get away from the dog, everyone laughs.

Self-enhancing humor makes us feel better. It works to improve one's own wellbeing by focusing on the positive aspects of life. It can be utilized in the workplace to inspire innovation and relieve stress.

Example: You're bored at work and decide to play a prank on your colleague, keeping another close friend in on the joke, and laughing loudly when the trick is discovered. The victim of the joke may laugh a little, and others may find the whole thing funny, but the prank was done primarily to make *you* feel good, not them.

Aggressive humor harms other people. It can be recognized as a style that disrespects others in the mistaken belief that it will benefit the joke-teller. Aggressive humor is often not humor at all, but hostility masked as humor with the intent of putting someone down so as to feel better about oneself.

Example: You're at a restaurant and the waiter messes up your order by accident. You call him over and, laughing sarcastically, say, "Oh, it's okay, son, words can be tough sometimes, huh? Would it help if I wrote everything down in crayon for you?"

Self-defeating humor harms oneself. It is used to amuse others while inflicting suffering to oneself. Self-deprecation is about putting yourself down, and while it can be funny if you're a professional comedian, the truth is it can often make others feel a bit uncomfortable, or at least they'll form a negative opinion of you and your self-esteem! Self-defeating humor can sometimes release tension, but it seldom makes anyone feel good.

Example: Your friend asks about how your blind date went and you laugh and say, "Well, she didn't cry and call the police when she saw me, so I'm counting that as a success."

According to the research, affiliative and self-enhancing humor styles are positive while aggressive self-defeating are negative humor styles. As you can imagine, **positive humor styles are more effective than negative ones at building relationships**. Positive humor enhances work cohesion and coping effectiveness, and negative humor decreases knowledge-sharing and trust. People whose partners use a positive (affiliative) style of humor during discussions feel closer to their partners and less stressed.

Maybe you're thinking, "That sounds great, but I'm just not a funny person." Don't worry, it is possible to learn to be funnier, whether it's at work or in your personal relationships. Here are a few tips:

- Don't deliberately try to be *funny*; instead, try to make observations about what is *true*. Often, good jokes rest on perceptions that everyone shares and relate to. To do this, you just need to be observant.
- Don't think of how to be a funny person, but think of what to say that will amuse other people, make them laugh, or put them at ease. Humor requires a lot of empathy!
- Unless you know a person extremely well, avoid making fun of them, excluding them, or pointing to vulnerabilities. There are much easier, less risky ways of getting a laugh.

- Avoid "inside jokes" that will only make part of your audience laugh, or else you may alienate some people.
- Avoid using humor to mask difficult conversations, such as giving hard feedback or acknowledging a serious negative situation. You may come across as insensitive, foolish, or tone-deaf.
- One easy way to bring more humor to others: take the initiative and find humor in your own life, even laughing at yourself. People who are positive, playful, and lighthearted are great to be around. Look for the funny side of things and laugh often yourself—it's contagious.

Being funny takes practice and a little risk-taking. If you're not used to being funny, start small. The next time you're in a social situation of any kind, try to pay attention to what is amusing to *you*, and see if you can share that more often with others. Look for absurdities, unexpected outcomes, or ridiculous situations that don't make sense. You don't have to "be funny" just to draw other people's attention to these little things!

Forget the Golden Rule, Use the Platinum Rule

We've all heard about the perennial Golden Rule that states *"Do unto others as you would have them do to you."* According to Dave Kerpen (author of the book *The Art of People*, 2016), this rule is simple and useful; however, it's limited because it doesn't recognize the fact that everyone is different, and, for example, while you might like to be treated a certain way, it doesn't mean that others want to be treated this way, too.

Kerpen devised his answer to this problem: the Platinum Rule: ***"Do unto others as they would want done to them."*** We are saying with this rule that our goal is not to give people what we ourselves want or apply to them our own frames of reference or values, but rather that will give them what they want according to *their* own frames of reference and values. Big difference!

Yes, it's important to teach others about how to treat you, but that's only one side of the coin. Because everyone has different difficulties, backgrounds, privileges, and blind spots, treating everyone the same is not really good enough. Kerpen's example is that, just because he likes strawberries and cream, it doesn't mean that using that as fish bait is going to get him anywhere when he goes fishing. He has to think about what *fish* like to eat! That's easy enough, but how do you actually know what people want? Well, you find out! That's what communication is for in the first place.

Here are a few pointers for applying the platinum rule, which may take a little practice:

Step 1: Take the initiative and first communicate how you want to be treated. To promote an environment where everyone feels empowered to speak up, one must first speak up for oneself. This may mean being very clear about your boundaries and asserting your limits by saying no when necessary.

Step 2: Listen and allow for a response. It is vital to set your ego aside and commit to actually learning more about the person in front of you. If someone has communicated to you that you've missed the mark and misunderstood them, accept that feedback gracefully without pushing back. After all, if someone says, "No, that's not right, *this* is what I want," then you can't argue with them, can you?

Step 3: Use empathy. It sometimes takes effort to understand what makes someone tick by simply talking with them, but don't let assumptions and bias get in the way. Importantly, you don't have to understand or agree with someone on their preferences and desires. You just have to acknowledge and speak to them. Start by acknowledging that other people can think, feel, and reason very differently from us—and that this isn't a problem!

Step 4: Stay curious. You can learn about how other people work by asking questions—and continuing to ask them even after you start to learn more about them:

What do they need?

What do they want?

How do they understand their situation?

What are they trying to achieve?

How do they conceptualize their problems?

You are not just trying to understand a single opinion or thought, but getting a more three-dimensional understanding of the whole framework they use to understand their world—even if it's very different from your own.

Let's take a look at some examples that will make this all clear.

You've been tasked with leading a newly assembled team at work, and a new hire is assigned to this team. This new employee is from another country that's culturally very different from your own. Even though you pride yourself on being an egalitarian, easygoing, and friendly kind of person, you realize that just because *you* value this way of working, it doesn't mean *they* will. You take the time to learn a little about the culture they've come from and realize that theirs is one that favors firmer and more authoritative leadership.

Though you personally would love a boss who tried to be friendly and relaxed with you, you also understand that they would prefer more formal and clear demarcations between your roles. Because you used the platinum rule, though, and not the golden rule, your interactions with them are so much more harmonious. Even though you don't quite agree with their perspective or even understand it, they still feel respected and understood by you.

Or let's say you are dating someone new and one day have your first disagreement. They're super upset because you haven't yet introduced them to your family; you're confused because they never even mentioned wanting to meet them, and the only reason you hadn't was because it hadn't even occurred to you yet. If you followed the golden rule, you might think, "Well, I don't see this as a big deal, so why are they making such a fuss?" and you'd fail to see that what you think is only half the story—because the way that they're conceiving the problem is entirely different. When you treat them in the way that they want to be treated (i.e., recognizing the things they care about even when you personally don't care about them), then your communication will be much smoother.

Give Proper Apologies

Even when we're doing our best and our intentions are as good as they can possibly be, we may still cause offense or say the wrong thing. **Knowing how to apologize is an invaluable people skill that may prove**

more useful one day than all the humor and charm in the world!

Ropy Lewicki has conducted interesting research and believes he's found the six-step formula for the best possible apology when you've messed up and want to make things right. The management and human resources professor at Ohio State University's Fisher College of Business claims that good apologies follow a universal narrative structure. He asked almost eight hundred participants to respond to different types of fictional apologies and noticed that the best ones tended to include certain key elements. He outlined these elements in a paper published in *Negotiation and Conflict Management Research* in 2016.

We've all heard terrible apologies ("I'm sorry you were offended …"), but here's how to craft one that will create more harmony:

1. Expressions of regret

You sincerely have to *be* sorry for what you've done. You need to show the other person that you're not apologizing because you're forced to, but because you genuinely are remorseful. Tone makes all the difference!

2. Explain what went wrong

Be careful here—explain, but don't make excuses or justify. What you want to do is explain your thought processes, outline what happened and why, and try to show the reasoning, even if flawed. You're not trying to get yourself off the hook or blame them, but rather show them that it wasn't really your intention to hurt them. Try to put them in your shoes without diminishing what you've done.

3. Acknowledge your responsibility

You need to be brave and accept that yes, things went wrong and it is, essentially, your fault. If you try to wriggle out of your culpability, blame someone or something else, or downplay the harm done, you're not taking responsibility, and you'll likely make the situation worse. Take responsibility squarely on yourself, no ifs, ands, or buts.

4. Declare your repentance

This simply means that you say you won't ever do it again, and really mean it. Feeling bad that you did something stupid and hurt someone is one thing, but it can go a long way to smoothing ruffled feathers if the other person genuinely believes you've learned a lesson and won't repeat the same thing again. Don't assume this goes without saying. You need to say it!

5. Offer to make things right

Even if you apologize sincerely, you might have left the other person with a real problem on their hands. Offer to help fix that problem or undo at least some of the trouble you've caused. It's great to say you won't do something again, but far better to take active steps toward making sure you don't. Pay for damages, or make a gesture that puts things right, even if just symbolically.

6. Ask for forgiveness

This is the very last thing you do. You apologize because it's the right thing to do, and not because you want to be quickly forgiven or absolved of your guilt. Many people think this is the most important part of an apology, but Lewicki thinks it's actually the least. He feels that what's more important is rebuilding trust, making things right, and actually learning to be better. Importantly, you only ask for forgiveness—you are not entitled to it, even if your apology is perfect. Don't keep asking, and don't make people feel guilty if they're unwilling to forgive. You'll only worsen matters if *you* suddenly act like the wronged party!

Though these steps seem like a lot, you can include them all pretty quickly if your offense was only minor (it's a bad idea to give an overwrought apology for a relatively small mistake!). Here's an example of a not-so-great apology, followed by that same apology that includes all six elements and will likely restore harmony far more quickly. The scenario is that you were looking after a friend's cat and left the door open when you shouldn't have, causing the cat to run away and promptly get run over by a car.

Written apology 1: "I'm sorry about what happened to your cat. He ran out on his own, and I couldn't help it. I'm completely torn up about it all and I feel horrible—please promise you won't be too upset? I couldn't live with myself if you didn't forgive me." (Notice how the focus is on them and their feelings, how no responsibility is taken, and how forgiveness is demanded rather than asked for?)

Written apology 2: "I am absolutely devastated about Bubbles and am so horrified about what's happened. I never intended any harm, but I wasn't paying close attention and didn't secure the front door latch, so it was slightly ajar, and that's when Bubbles must have slipped out. It was an accident, but nevertheless it was completely my fault and I accept total responsibility for what happened. I know there's no way I can bring Bubbles back, but I can assure you I will never be making this mistake again. For one thing, I've fixed the front door latch! I hope you'll let me pay for all the vet services, and though it doesn't make things right, I've also sent some flowers to you and your family. Again, I'm sorry and hope one day you can forgive me." (All six components present!)

Lewicki did other experiments on apologies and wanted to understand whether failures of competence (i.e., it was a mistake) or failures of integrity (i.e., you knowingly did something wrong) were affected by these six elements in an apology. In experiments where participants were considering the apology of a job applicant who had done something wrong in their last job, it turns out that the *reason* for the problem mattered. "Overall, though, the two studies showed that participants were, in fact, less likely to accept an apology [. . .] when the job applicant was shown as having a lack of integrity versus lack of competence," said Lewicki.

So, an honest mistake is more easily forgiven than a malicious choice to cause harm or act immorally. If you're apologizing for the latter, you're going to need to work extra hard to be forgiven!

Takeaways:

- There are many ways to assert your own boundaries and limits without encroaching on others'. Try the stuck record technique (calmly repeating your limit without budging), the "positive no" (reiterate what you are saying yes to) negative assertion or negative enquiry (accepting and enquiring about criticism).
- The DESC model can help you stand up for yourself. **D**escribe the facts of the situation, **E**xpress how you are being affected, suggest a specific **S**olution, then finish with a **C**onclusion/consequences, i.e. what will happen if the behavior is changed and what will happen if it isn't.

- Humor is useful, but it needs to be the right kind. Positive humor styles (especially affiliative humor) are better for relationships. Avoid self-enhancing, aggressive or self-defeating humor styles.
- Use the platinum rule: Do unto others as they would want done to them. Listen, be empathetic and stay curious about other people's perspectives, even and especially if they differ from yours. Ask what *they* want and need, and how they conceptualize of you, themselves, and the situation.
- A good apology needs a few necessary elements: expression of regret, explanation of what went wrong, taking responsibility, repentance, offer for reparations, and a request for forgiveness.

Chapter 5: Dealing with Conflict and Disagreement

Argue Better by "Steel Manning"

In our final chapter, we'll consider a few useful techniques for those times in life when communication becomes conflicted, hostile, or confusing. Disagreement doesn't have to be a problem—if we possess the social skills needed to navigate it properly! In an Atlantic Article, Conor Friedershof explains how **steel manning is the "highest form of disagreement."**

How does one argue effectively? You might have heard of "straw man fallacy," which is the act of exaggerating or distorting someone's point of view to win an argument. For example, a person critical of vegan diets might claim that vegans are all easily influenced young people with no understanding of nutrition, and they all want everyone to eat measly salads all day long. Such a person might feel that they've won a point against the vegans as they are in this description, but there's one big problem: that description is not accurate.

There is an opposite of this technique that's actually far more helpful to use in arguments: the steel man technique. Instead of constructing an unflattering and easy-to-defeat image of your opponent and then destroying that, "steel manning" entails constructing the *best* version of the opposing side's argument before engaging with it. It's being charitable and deliberately patching up the flaws in the other side's argument so they can come up with the most effective counterargument to your position.

You might be wondering why you'd go to all this effort. Well, the steel-manning approach avoids a "you versus me" scenario. By first siding with the opposing side and reasoning in their terms, you demonstrate that you are genuinely interested in and understand their arguments. This will greatly increase the likelihood of them returning the favor, and suddenly, you are two respectful peers who are having an intelligent discussion, rather than two enemies who are flinging mud at one another. Even if you arrive at no real resolution, you have done something important: maintained respectful and harmonious relations.

Etiquette matters, perhaps in arguments more than at any other time. You're not doing it to be selfless, however. Steel manning ennobles both you and the other person and makes the best of your interaction, wherever it goes. Let's take a close look at the three steps of the steel man approach, with an example.

Step 1: Create the best version of your opponent's argument by breaking it down

First, just set your own ideas aside for a moment, not unlike what you'd do in active listening. Focus on what the other person is actually saying, not what you *think* they're saying (clean language will help here!). Be curious and empathetic, as though you were simply trying to find out more about a new person or culture, or even an alien race.

What is the main point they're making? How are they supporting that line of argument? Can you identify the worldview, points of reference, attitudes, fears, beliefs, and motivations behind the argument? Can you find any weak points, gaps, or flaws in this argument?

As you do this, your intent is purely to understand—you're not looking for a *gotcha!* moment. We're also not trying to see if we agree. Just observe and understand, that's all.

Example: You look at the vegans again and try to understand their position. They are actually acting from a moral and not a practical perspective, and they are making claims about the duty of humans to not create needless suffering in others. You start to see that nutrition actually has nothing to do with their core line of argument.

Step 2: Help them steel man their argument

Remember that people will never accept criticism or feedback from people they don't believe actually understand their position in the first place. If you go in with a straw man, you convince nobody and achieve nothing. You may disagree with someone, but disagree with the best version of their claim, and everyone wins.

Ask the other person questions to clarify (again, not to catch out!), then restate what they've said in your own words to show you've understood (this may take a few tries). Present them with a summary of what you've been told that they themselves would agree with.

Only when you've arrived at a picture of their point of view that you both agree is fair and reflective, then you can start drawing attention to points they may not themselves have noticed. Do you see the value of steel manning now? If you've begun in good faith and worked together until this point, the other person is going to be far more interested in seeing what you point out. We are not just being contrarian; we are collaborating with them. It's as though we say, "I respect you as a person and I want to make sure you have the best possible argument here. Let's help each other do that."

Example: You offer your vegan conversation partner your understanding of their position—i.e., the steel man version—and focus on the moral core of the argument. You say that this means that eating for health may be a secondary concern. They agree.

Step 3: Argue on your counterpart's behalf

This takes enormous creativity, intelligence, and maturity. Don't just look at the other person's perspective from the outside. Get inside it and feel it for yourself. If you do this, you can see with crystal clarity the reasons why the person believes as they do, and everything that is standing in the way of them agreeing with you (if this is what you in fact want). You will never know an issue as deeply as when you deliberately and genuinely occupy both "sides."

Example: Once you really feel like you *get* the vegan's arguments, you more properly understand their behavior and the things they say. But now, when you make the criticism that veganism as a way of life seems nutritionally a little suspect, they are less likely to argue—after all, you have both agreed together that being nutritionally sound is *not* the core aim of the philosophy! However, coming at this issue in this way means the other side can actually hear it. Ignorantly saying, "Vegans know nothing about nutrition," only creates more tension and discord.

Importantly, we could reverse this argument and instead have the vegan hear the omnivore's position, going through the three steel-manning steps in the same way. What matters is that neither party is approaching the debate to win, to beat down their "opponent," or to prove themselves superior. And because of this, they *both* leave the discussion as winners, with intact self-esteem and possibly more robust arguments going forward.

Sure, you probably can't imagine going through this whole process with every minor disagreement. Steel manning works best for high-stakes and very emotional topics, but can also be used in more everyday ways here and there. You may simply be more aware of this dynamic in everyday conversations and refuse to engage in dialogues where your argument is willfully misconstrued. Or you might get into the habit of reminding yourself, "Everyone's opinion makes sense to them. If I don't understand, it's just because I don't yet see how it makes sense." It's a choice to assume that people are sane, broadly good, and are behaving in a way according to their principles.

Steel manning in arguments is about dignity—yours and the other person's—and shifting your mindset when it comes to the *purpose* of dialogue. Steel manning holds everyone to a higher standard and takes ego out of it. Think of it this way: you can win or you can convince. You can stubbornly boast or you can understand.

Use this technique often enough and you will discover that you are far more ready to change your own opinion than you first realized—and this is not "losing" an argument but gaining so much more!

Dealing with Aggressive People: the Fogging Technique

Let's be honest, no matter how cool, calm, and collected you are, occasionally in life you will encounter someone who is . . . not. Once someone has become actively hostile or rude, it can be incredibly difficult to pull the conversation back to *terra firma*. In an earlier chapter, we explored how to be assertive by using the "stuck record" technique and reiterating our boundaries calmly but firmly. Think of the fogging trick as taking things a step further.

This technique was first developed by Manuel J. Smith in his book *When I Say No, I Feel Guilty* (1975). To put it simply, this is an assertiveness technique that allows us to respond calmly to someone who is aggressive toward us. **Fogging is all about**

giving people a minimal, calm response using terms that are pacifying but not defensive. Imagine fog: it's there, but you can't exactly fight against it or nail it down.

Fogging involves neutrally agreeing with any truth contained in statements, even if it is critical. Because you are not responding by being defensive or argumentative, the confrontation will eventually end because the desired effect is not being achieved. There is nothing to push back against or grab hold of.

Fogging is not just pacifism or escaping. The idea is that when the atmosphere is calmer, it will be easier to talk about the issues rationally. Before then, there's no point in actually engaging, so don't.

The technique is simple. First and foremost, pay attention to *what* the other person is saying, regardless of *how* they are saying it. When something they say is true, rather than becoming defensive or argumentative, we simply state in a calm and clear tone that it is, in fact, true.

For example, when the aggressive person says, "What were you thinking when you acted so stupidly in that meeting? You were embarrassing me in front of our coworkers!" rather than replying with something equally aggressive or defensive, you could try to "fog" them by responding, "You're right. My behavior was pretty stupid a while ago. I understand that my actions were really embarrassing."

You don't add anything or take away anything. You agree with what is factually correct without going on the defensive or upping the emotional stakes. The other person may try again, but eventually it will seem pointless to keep coming for you since you've acknowledged their grievance. If, however, you denied or deflected or got aggressive yourself, the conflict could get even more heated.

In a way, fogging is not all that dissimilar from steel manning. If we can have the strength of character to affirm that there is a kernel of truth in even the criticisms leveled at us, we are responding in effect to the best possible version of that criticism. We immediately elevate the discussion rather than bring it down to aggression or defense.

Although it might be the last thing you feel like doing in the heat of the moment, fogging is actually a great assertiveness technique and can be used to de-escalate conflict.

Basically, the best way to be in the face of aggression is calm and neutral. Not passive, not aggressive, just neutral—like fog. Don't feed the aggression, don't respond to it, don't fight with it. Ironically, this puts you in more control of the situation, not less.

The technique is simple:

1. Listen closely for any truth in what is being said.
2. Repeat this truth as **calmly and neutrally as possible**.
3. Don't add any new information, and don't respond to exaggerations, distortions, or lies. Just ignore those.
4. Importantly, maintain calmness, even if the other person is aggressive.

People in call centers or those managing complaints often need to master this skill. For example:

A: I was promised the builders would be finished by Thursday afternoon, and now it's already *Saturday* and they're *still* busy!

B: You're right, we did agree to a Thursday afternoon, but despite it being Saturday, they're not finished yet.

A: This is unacceptable! Totally unacceptable.

B: Yes, I can see how this is not something you're happy with.

A: Damn straight I'm not happy. I had plans for this weekend, and now they're ruined.

B: I recognize that. It's an unacceptable situation, and you've had to change your plans. That's on us.

A: Yes, well, it *is* your fault. But I need them to be finished now.

B: I understand that. I'm going to do everything in my power to make sure we make this a priority. They need to be finished as soon as possible.

A: Exactly. Thank you. Sorry for yelling, it's been a long week. Please just sort it out.

B: Absolutely. Thank you for being patient.

The conversation above is really about energy. Person A begins with aggression, and Person B responds with calm. A responds with more aggression, and B again responds with calm. Gradually, A's aggression drains away in the face of B's calm "fog." They're still not exactly happy, but the aggression has lessened.

Notice how this process is similar to giving a good apology—we need to accept responsibility but without beating ourselves up or defending ourselves.

Though simple, this technique is not always easy. The biggest problem is to not get upset and defensive ourselves. Maintaining calm when we feel attacked is difficult, but it's a powerful way to dial back that fight-or-flight, high-stakes feeling. You don't have to apologize, explain, justify, or elaborate. Just imagine that a pile of mud has been flung at you, and your job is simply to pick out the small bits of gold that might be in it. Don't get distracted by the mud!

It's also a good idea to acknowledge how the other person feels, but be careful about stating the obvious or putting words into people's mouths. Likewise, fogging works as a temporary way to de-escalate tension. Once tension is lowered, either pull back or try to re-engage again. Nothing can be more frustrating than a person who is just a blank wall and keeps repeating what you say!

Turn Conflict into Compassion with the Ransberger Pivot

When conversing with someone who has a different view from ours, our first knee-jerk reaction may be to contradict or correct them. This could drive the discussion to become intense, personal, and ineffective. **If we *really* want to convince someone with our point of view, though, something that can come in handy is the Ransberger Pivot, which is almost a way to "win an argument without arguing."**

Created in 1982 by Ray Ransberger and Marshall Fritz, this technique helps you find common ground with an intellectual "opponent" so you can maintain conversational harmony. Using the pivot is simple, and as you'll see, it has a lot in common with some of the other techniques already discussed.

First, **stop talking and listen carefully to what they are saying.** Make it your mission to learn what matters to them and why. As in the DESC model, make eye contact and seek to understand before wanting to be understood.

Second, **voice a point of agreement and admit misunderstanding.** Actively look for points that you agree on as though you are building a bridge to reach one another. Reiterate how you are not, fundamentally, on the same team. Literally say, "I agree . . ." as often as possible. If you find out that you misunderstood or misinterpreted something they said, be honest and admit it. They may be more willing to reciprocate later in the conversation if you admit an error or mistake. Remember to *fight with and not against*. You are not identifying *who* is right, but *what* is right. If you discover that you're actually in error, gracefully admit it and move on swiftly.

Lastly, **follow up.** Now that you've reframed the conversation, you're on the same page about the problem and want the same positive outcome. This is the time to start discussing how your idea will help you both solve the problem. Talk about solutions, ways forward, and plans. Remember to keep your common goal in mind and stay respectful.

Using the Ransberger Pivot is effective in putting people on opposite sides of an issue and bringing them together, avoiding a heated discussion. It shifts from a combative to a cooperative environment. There is suddenly a lot less to argue about when both people agree. In addition, it validates the other person rather than attacking them; you can end the conversation as friends rather than enemies.

Dale Carnegie, author of the 1936 classic *How to Win Friends and Influence People*, once said, "A man convinced against his will is of the same opinion still." In discussion, people want to feel important, seen, and understood. This is an emotional need, not a cognitive or intellectual one. When people push against us, we push back—that's human nature. So, if you frame any conversation as an *attack*, expect that people will respond to it with *defense*.

The Ransberger Pivot is about getting out of this me-versus-you framework and putting both people on the same side. When you abandon the idea of winning an argument, you realize that you don't actually need to have a winner and a loser, and it's not *necessary* for someone to feel humiliated, chastened, or corrected. The technique helps you get to that frame of mind sooner.

As with the other techniques of this kind, you don't need to go all out with every tiny disagreement. In everyday life, simply make the conscious effort to focus on what you agree on, rather than dwell on what you don't agree on. Keep asking yourself, **in what way am I and the other person the same? In what way do we want the same thing?** Then focus on that.

Most human beings have a strong sense of fairness and justice, most want to protect children, to reward the deserving, and to support the things they believe benefit society. Use "chunking up" techniques (as discussed earlier) to zoom out until you find the bigger picture that you can both agree on. This dissolves the feeling of enmity and makes your differences a mere detail, something practical to work out. If you first establish that you are on the same team, then you are like two people working together on a puzzle, rather than warriors mutually trying to kill one another.

One very important point: this technique is about emotion, not facts and logic. Get on the same page emotionally. If all that means is you politely and sincerely "agree to disagree," that's still progress!

When Resolving Conflict, Use the "Feel, Felt, Found" Approach

Bearing in mind the importance of emotional understanding in conflict, let's take a look at the Feel, Felt, Found approach, which is a well-known objection-handling strategy among salespeople. Despite its background, this technique can also be used in addressing conflict with family and friends (Romanova, 2019, Moscow State Linguistic University).

The typical wording of feel, felt, found is as follows:

"I understand how you **feel**." This is meant to show the person that you have heard them and can empathize with them.

"I know someone who had a similar situation and **felt** the same way." Tell them about someone else who felt the same way they did at first. You're assuring the person that they're not alone and that things can improve.

"We **found** that this worked best" Explain to them how that individual discovered the solution that fixed the problem.

You might not always have the time or energy for a more elaborate approach, or it simply may not be appropriate. But the feel, felt, found technique can be deployed quickly and easily almost any time. Quickly create empathy by acknowledging how the other person feels (note, this comes *first!*), gently shift the issue into more objective territory by relating that emotion to someone else, then finish off by pointing to what's worked in the past to resolve the current issue.

Here are a few more examples to see this technique in action:

With a client expressing concerns over a project time frame:

"I completely get that you're **feel**ing nervous about how long the first drafts are taking to be completed. My other clients have **felt** that way in the past before. What I've **found**, however, is that they often feel better once they see at least one or two mockups and can envision how the project will turn out."

With a stressed-out family member:

"I know you must **feel** so overwhelmed right now with planning everything for this trip. I certainly **felt** that way when I was planning our big holiday last year. I've **found** that slowing down and just paying attention to the very next task you need to focus on makes a big difference."

With a customer who has a complaint about your product:

"I can see you're disappointed about XYZ's performance. We had another customer just this morning who experienced the same thing. He discovered that allowing the battery to power down completely now and then got rid of the problem." (In this example, you can see that a similar effect is possible even if you don't use the exact words feel, felt, and found).

A word of warning, though: this approach, like the fogging technique, is designed for use in short bursts. You've probably called a customer care line before or made a complaint, only to encounter someone who talked to you robotically and seemed to deflect every point you raised. Somehow, being *told* again and again, "I understand how you feel," just didn't make things better! You needed someone to demonstrate that they understood and take meaningful action to help you.

It has to be genuine, and the anecdotes you raise must have some real and believable connection to the person you're talking to. In other words, this tactic comes from the sales world, and *it shows*! Don't say, "I know how you feel" if you sincerely don't and have made zero effort to empathize. Likewise, your suggested course of action should not be a brush-off, but something that can really help the other person.

This technique could be used to put people's minds at ease and address reservations (thereby convincing and persuading them), or it can be used to smooth over misunderstandings or gently bring people round to solutions rather than dwell on grievances. You could combine this trick with fogging, or use both negative enquiry and negative assertion when someone is approaching you with criticism or complaint. For example:

"I can see you **feel** angry with me right now for not fixing this problem for you. You're right that this incident could have been handled better (fogging). What exactly did you hope I would be able to do for you today (negative enquiry)? I once had a colleague who **felt** how you did. We found that when we communicated things by email, we understood each other a lot better. Might that help here?"

A few things to remember when using this technique:

- Try as hard as you can not to be dismissive. Your attitude is more calm, neutral, and in control rather than, "This isn't important; I'm brushing you off."
- It can be useful to point to a time when you felt what they did, but it's usually better to talk about how someone else felt what they did. You don't want to make it seem like you are inserting your own feelings or making everything about you.
- When showing empathy, use phrases like, "that makes sense" or "I can see why you feel that way."
- Remember your platinum rule and frame potential solutions and resolutions from their perspective. What would help *them* feel better right now?
- If you are genuinely out of your depth and can't think of a truthful way to use this approach, don't. Don't merely *pretend* to have everything under

control! Not every situation can be de-escalated, and there may be situations where you personally cannot offer legitimate help; in this case, be honest and offer apologies or make amends.

Use the Agreement Frame

Our final conflict resolution strategy comes to us from the world of NLP (Neurolinguistic Programming). NLP is an approach to personal development and psychotherapy created by Richard Bandler and John Grinder in the 1970s. The Agreement Frame is an offshoot of this approach; **it's a language structure that allows us to gracefully disagree with and persuade someone *without destroying rapport.*** This is what we have been trying to do with every single technique discussed in this book so far. In way, the agreement frame is one that underpins the entire approach we've been trying to cultivate throughout: one of collaboration, understanding, empathy, and respect.

The technique is pretty simple. The important words to use are "I agree/respect/appreciate," followed by "and." We begin by saying those mentioned

I-statements and then we express the other person's model of the universe or perspective on the circumstance. Then we say "and," then our intended outcome, and finally the other person's desired outcome.

For example:

"**I respect** your concerns, **and** you may want to be aware of that . . ."

"**I appreciate** that you're saying this because you sincerely care, **and** what's most important here is that we . . ."

"**I agree** that from your point of view, this makes the most sense, **and** I invite you to consider that . . ."

The Agreement Frame eliminates opposition from others, primarily because it doesn't use combative language like "but." Imagine that the word "but" basically cancels out everything you've said before. The agreement frame keeps people interested in what we are saying and leaves them open to fresh ideas.

Interestingly, it does not recommend the use of "I understand" because it can provoke an argument that you don't really understand. "Oh, sure, I understand" can come across as extremely condescending and dismissive.

When we instead say, "I agree/respect/appreciate," it's more believable, and the other person's thinking shifts into a receptive condition to hear how we agree with them. This receptive condition also makes them more open to our suggestions. Let's take a closer look.

The expanded structure of the frame goes like this:

YOU AGREE > YOU ACKNOLEDGE THEIR WORLD MODEL > "AND" > YOU ACKNOLWEDGE YOUR DESIRED OUTCOME > YOU FINISH WITH THEIR DESIRED OUTCOME

Looking at that, you can see that the intention is to maintain rapport while still disagreeing. You literally put your views together in the same expression, but without language to show any problem. Starting out with "I agree" is like a signpost that primes the listener that there is no threat coming. Doing this alone is extremely effective at making others more receptive to what we say.

The secret is to maintain rapport and to almost sandwich your request or contentious opinion. Look above at the structure: YOU AKCNOWLEDGE YOUR

DESIRED OUTCOME is wedged in only after you demonstrate that you grasp and respect *their* desired outcome. Then things proceed smoothly. Compare the following:

Conversation 1:

"We have loads more to do on this. We're going to need to do overtime."

"Hmmm . . . I'm pretty exhausted. I don't know if I can manage overtime right now."

"*Really*?" (Person is annoyed, and there's a sudden feeling of conflict).

Conversation 2:

"We have loads more to do on this; if we want to get everything done by our deadline, we're going to need to do overtime."

"I agree. We're swamped! And I think if we have some much-needed rest right now, we'll be able to get everything done by our deadline."

Can you spot the agreement frame structure? This is not unlike non-violent communication where we assert our own needs, boundaries, and desires without arousing any resistance in the other person.

Note also that here, there is a subtle Ransberger Pivot being used, in that the person ends by mentioning their common shared goal. It's hard to imagine anyone responding negatively to conversation 2—the disagreement is still there, but there isn't any hostility, aggression, or negativity.

The agreement frame is a simple technique that runs very deep. It's an approach that says, "I am confident enough and respect you enough to disagree with you without it being a problem." Even if you can't quite remember how to construct an agreement frame in the moment, try to remember simply to banish this word "but" from your vocabulary and simply replace it with "and" (that goes for all related words, like however, yet, although . . .).

In truth, sometimes it may feel like a stretch to say, "I agree," and doing so could come across as phony. But you can use other words, such as "I respect" or "I appreciate." Remembering that much of conflict resolution is about emotions; it's more about the energy and attitude you're conveying than the literal words you're saying. For that matter, watch your tone, body language, and facial expression when you speak, too.

Each of us processes information differently. But we are all the same in that we don't respond well when our viewpoint is dismissed out of hand, and somebody comes along to correct, belittle, or downplay that viewpoint. Sometimes, however, you don't necessarily need to dig down deep into another person's mental filters and personal beliefs. All you need to do is respectfully acknowledge it, behave as though it matters and is as important as your own, and demonstrate that you're willing to accommodate it. Wouldn't you like others to take the same approach with you?

The big insight is that we don't have to make others wrong to express what we think is right. When your goal is rapport, flow and connection, then almost all conflict is removed. Sure, you may still disagree, but you can do so from a place of mutual respect and understanding. So, ironically, the world's best conflict resolution experts and mediators are those who begin every encounter expressly *not* focusing on the conflict at hand. This is easily said but quick tricky to put into practice. Once you get a taste for how this mindset shift completely changes your social interactions, though, you'll never look back.

Takeaways

- Arguments are sometimes inevitable but we can argue best if we use "steel manning" rather than attacking a strawman. Create the best version of your opponent's argument by breaking it down, then help them build that argument, actively arguing on your counterpart's behalf. You will more quickly reach harmonious agreement, or at least disagree more civilly.
- Use the fogging technique to manage people who are aggressive or unreasonable. By giving people a minimal, calm response that they cannot easily engage with, you defuse tension. Listen carefully for a kernel of truth, repeat the truth calmly and neutrally, but don't add any new information and keep maintaining calm.
- The Ransberger pivot is a way to "win an argument without arguing." Listen carefully to start, look for points of commonality, and keep returning to any ways in which you and the other person are actually on the same page.
- The "feel, felt, found" technique is another a simple way to mitigate conflict. Acknowledge how they *feel*, point to

another person who has *felt* similarly in the past, then show what you have *found* works based on how this person managed the issue.

- Finally, the agreement frame allows us to gracefully disagree with someone without destroying rapport. Use terms like *I respect*, *I appreciate* and *I agree* to signal an intention to cooperate. Agree, acknowledge their position, and acknowledge both your desired outcomes, using "and" rather than "but."

Summary Guide

CHAPTER 1: BUILD YOUR SOCIAL AWARENESS

- No matter who you are, it's always possible to improve your people skills and become a more charming and more likeable conversationalist.
- Start by building more social awareness. If eye contact is often awkward or uncomfortable, try the triangle technique: Draw an imaginary inverted triangle on the other person's face around their eyes and mouth. During the conversation, change your gaze every five to ten seconds.
- Be aware of proxemics as a nonverbal mode of communication. Intimate, social, personal or public space are used in different contexts and can signal intentions, with people regulating their social closeness by changing their physical proximity.
- "Perceptual positions" can help you build empathy and switch perspectives. First position is seeing the world through our eyes, second position is seeing the world through someone else's eyes, and third

position is seeing the world through a neutral observer's eyes. You can gain insight into a situation by adopting each position in turn.

- To be a better and more active listener, paraphrase, clarify and summarize. Avoid judging, interpreting through your own perspective or interrupting, and simply listen.

CHAPTER 2: THE POWER OF EMPATHY

- Empathy is a nonnegotiable ingredient in genuine, connected interactions, and one easy way to create it is to give compliments. Make it authentic, meaningful to the person receiving it and specific, avoiding insincere exaggeration or vague niceties that don't speak to the person's values.
- Learn to recognize "bids for attention" because when you "turn toward" these unspoken requests for connection and validation, you deepen and strengthen relationships of all kinds, and respond with empathy. Turning against or away from these requests does the opposite.

- Practice the art of nonviolent communication by using four simple steps: first, observe without judgment or interpretation. Second, express how you feel without blame or making anyone responsible. Third, express your needs plainly and assertively, without implicating the other person. Finally, calmly express a specific request that stems from the previous three steps, without entitlement or force. This will make any difficult or emotional conversation infinitely easier.
- Use language softeners. Softer language can help foster trust, empathy, and likeability in all social situations. Use modal verbs and qualifiers, focus on the positive, be mindful of your word choice and use a gentler, more respectful and unhurried style to communicate a friendly willingness to cooperate.

CHAPTER 3: BETTER CONVERSATION SKILLS

- One useful conversational skill is chunking, where you vary the level of information you get coming back to you.

This way, you can reach an agreement, acquire more and correct detail, or even persuade people to move from one plane of thought to another. Chunk up to gain a broader view everyone can agree on, and chunk down to find detail. Move from general to specific, keeping the other person's reactions in mind.

- Use clean language to discover, explore and work with people's metaphors without "contaminating" them. Listen for metaphors used, ask questions about them and continue the conversation using the same language and imagery to show your understanding.

- Use the HPM technique to always have something to say in conversations. Talk about history (a past experience) philosophy (your feelings on it) and a metaphor (describe both with a vivid metaphor). Keep is short, sweet and natural.

- Use signposting and transitional words to tell your listeners where your story is going. Signal what is coming and link your ideas logically using words that guide your listener's understanding.

- Use conversational threading. Listen out for emotional hooks and pursue the conversation in that direction. Follow the most exciting or interesting leads and return to old, unexplored ones when conversation flags or ideas run out.

CHAPTER 4: NAVIGATING BOUNDARIES

- There are many ways to assert your own boundaries and limits without encroaching on others'. Try the stuck record technique (calmly repeating your limit without budging), the "positive no" (reiterate what you are saying yes to) negative assertion or negative enquiry (accepting and enquiring about criticism).
- The DESC model can help you stand up for yourself. **D**escribe the facts of the situation, **E**xpress how you are being affected, suggest a specific **S**olution, then finish with a **C**onclusion/consequences, i.e. what will happen if the behavior is changed and what will happen if it isn't.
- Humor is useful, but it needs to be the right kind. Positive humor styles (especially affiliative humor) are better for relationships. Avoid self-enhancing,

aggressive or self-defeating humor styles.

- Use the platinum rule: Do unto others as they would want done to them. Listen, be empathetic and stay curious about other people's perspectives, even and especially if they differ from yours. Ask what *they* want and need, and how they conceptualize of you, themselves, and the situation.

- A good apology needs a few necessary elements: expression of regret, explanation of what went wrong, taking responsibility, repentance, offer for reparations, and a request for forgiveness.

CHAPTER 5: DEALING WITH CONFLICT AND DISAGREEMENT

- Arguments are sometimes inevitable but we can argue best if we use "steel manning" rather than attacking a strawman. Create the best version of your opponent's argument by breaking it down, then help them build that argument, actively arguing on your counterpart's behalf. You will more quickly reach harmonious agreement, or at least disagree more civilly.

- Use the fogging technique to manage people who are aggressive or unreasonable. By giving people a minimal, calm response that they cannot easily engage with, you defuse tension. Listen carefully for a kernel of truth, repeat the truth calmly and neutrally, but don't add any new information and keep maintaining calm.

- The Ransberger pivot is a way to "win an argument without arguing." Listen carefully to start, look for points of commonality, and keep returning to any ways in which you and the other person are actually on the same page.

- The "feel, felt, found" technique is another a simple way to mitigate conflict. Acknowledge how they *feel*, point to another person who has *felt* similarly in the past, then show what you have *found* works based on how this person managed the issue.

- Finally, the agreement frame allows us to gracefully disagree with someone without destroying rapport. Use terms like *I respect*, *I appreciate* and *I agree* to signal an intention to cooperate. Agree, acknowledge their position, and acknowledge both your desired outcomes, using "and" rather than "but."

Milton Keynes UK
Ingram Content Group UK Ltd.
UKHW040957180923
428892UK00003B/36